The Narcissist And the Psychopath In the Workplace

2nd EDITION

Sam Vaknin

The Author is NOT a Mental Health Professional.

"Malignant Self-love: Narcissism Revisited" is based on correspondence since 1996 with hundreds of people diagnosed with Narcissistic and Antisocial Personality Disorders (narcissists and psychopaths) and with thousands of family members, friends, therapists, and colleagues.

Editing and Design:
Lidija Rangelovska

Narcissus Publications, Skopje 2015

Warning and Disclaimer

The contents of this book are not meant to substitute for professional help and counselling. The readers are discouraged from using it for diagnostic or therapeutic ends. The diagnosis and treatment of Narcissistic Personality Disorder can only be done by professionals specifically trained and qualified to do so – which the author is not. The author is NOT a mental health professional.

© 1999-2015 Copyright Lidija Rangelovska

All rights reserved. This book, or any part thereof, may not be used or reproduced in any manner without written permission from:

Lidija Rangelovska – write to: malignantselflove@gmail.com

To get FREE updates of this book JOIN the Narcissism Study List. To JOIN, visit our Web sites:
http://www.narcissistic-abuse.com/narclist.html or
http://groups.yahoo.com/group/narcissisticabuse

Visit the Author's Web site   http://www.narcissistic-abuse.com
Facebook   http://www.facebook.com/samvaknin
YouTube channel   http://www.youtube.com/samvaknin

Buy other books and video lectures about pathological narcissism and relationships with abusive narcissists and psychopaths here:
http://www.narcissistic-abuse.com/thebook.html

CONTENTS

Pathological Narcissism - An Overview
A Primer on Narcissism and the Narcissistic Personality Disorder (NPD)
The Narcissist's Entitlement of Routine
Pathological Narcissism - A Dysfunction or a Blessing?
The Narcissist's Confabulated Life
The Cult of the Narcissist
Bibliography

The Narcissist in the Workplace
The Narcissist in the Workplace
Narcissism in the Boardroom
The Professions of the Narcissist

Narcissists in Positions of Authority
Narcissistic Leaders
Narcissists in Positions of Authority

Workplace Bullying
Bully at Work - Interview with Tim Field
Narcissism in the Workplace - Online conference transcript HealthyPlace.com

Celebrity Narcissists
The Narcissist's Addiction to Fame and Celebrity
Mistreating Celebrities - An Interview Granted to Superinteressante Magazine in Brazil
Acquired Situational Narcissism

Narcissists and God - The Religious Narcissist
For the Love of God
The Narcissist and Social Institutions

Guide to Coping with Narcissists and Psychopaths

The Author

Online index
Go here: http://samvak.tripod.com/siteindex.html

The Narcissist And the Psychopath In the Workplace

Pathological Narcissism – An Overview

A Primer on Narcissism
And Narcissistic Personality Disorder (NPD)

Most narcissists are men. This is why I use male pronouns throughout this book. Of course, there are women narcissists as well.

The Risks of Self-diagnosis and Labelling

Narcissistic Personality Disorder (NPD) is a *disease*. It is defined *only* by and in the Diagnostic and Statistical Manual (DSM). All other "definitions" and compilations of "criteria" are irrelevant and very misleading.

People go around putting together lists of traits and behaviours (usually based on their experience with one person who was never officially diagnosed as a narcissist) and deciding that these lists constitute the essence or definition of narcissism.

People are erroneously using the term "narcissist" to describe every type of abuser, or obnoxious and uncouth person. That is wrong. Not all abusers are narcissists.

Only a qualified mental health diagnostician can determine whether someone suffers from Narcissistic Personality Disorder (NPD) and this, following lengthy tests and personal interviews.

It is true enough that narcissists can mislead even the most experienced professional, let alone a layman. The same signs and symptoms may apply with equal force to several psychological problems. Differentiating between them takes years of learning, specialized training, qualifications, and experience.

What is Pathological Narcissism?

Pathological narcissism is a life-long pattern of traits and behaviours which signify infatuation and obsession with one's self to the exclusion of all others and the egotistic and ruthless pursuit of one's gratification, dominance, and ambition.

As distinct from healthy narcissism, which we all possess, pathological narcissism is maladaptive, rigid, persisting, and causes significant distress and functional impairment.

Pathological narcissism was first described in detail by Freud in his essay "On Narcissism" (1914). Other major contributors to the study of narcissism are: Melanie Klein, Karen Horney, Franz Kohut, Otto Kernberg, Theodore Millon, Elsa Roningstam, J.G. Gunderson, and Robert Hare.

What is Narcissistic Personality Disorder (NPD)?

Narcissistic Personality Disorder (NPD) is not a new psychological construct. In previous centuries it was called "egotism" or "megalomania". It is an extreme form of pathological narcissism. It is a Cluster B (dramatic, emotional, or erratic) personality disorder.

The other Cluster B personality disorders are Borderline Personality Disorder (BPD), Antisocial Personality Disorder (APD, or psychopathy and sociopathy), and Histrionic Personality Disorder (HPD).

Narcissistic Personality Disorder (NPD) made its first appearance as a mental health diagnosis in the DSM (Diagnostic and Statistical Manual) III-TR in 1980.

Diagnostic Criteria

The ICD-10 (International Classification of Diseases), published by the World Health Organization (WHO) in Geneva (1992), regards Narcissistic Personality Disorder (NPD) as *"a personality disorder that fits none of the specific rubrics"*. It relegates it to the category "Other Specific Personality Disorders" together with the eccentric, "haltlose", immature, passive-aggressive, and psychoneurotic personality disorders and types.

The American Psychiatric Association, based in Washington D.C., USA, publishes the Diagnostic and Statistical Manual of Mental Disorders, fourth edition, Text Revision (DSM IV-TR, 2000) and fifth edition (2013), where it provides the diagnostic criteria for Narcissistic Personality Disorder [301.81, p. 669].

Both editions of the DSM define Narcissistic Personality Disorder (NPD) as *"a pervasive pattern of grandiosity (in fantasy or behaviour), need for admiration, and lack of empathy, beginning by early adulthood and present in various contexts"*, such as family life and work.

Five or more of the DSM's nine diagnostic criteria must be met for a diagnosis of Narcissistic Personality Disorder (NPD) to be rendered.

Proposed Amended Diagnostic Criteria for Narcissistic Personality Disorder (NPD)

[In the text below, I have proposed modifications to the language of these criteria to incorporate current knowledge about this disorder. My modifications appear in italics.]

[My amendments do not constitute a part of the text of the DSM IV-TR, nor is the American Psychiatric Association (APA) associated with them in any way.]

- Feels grandiose and self-important (e.g., exaggerates accomplishments, talents, *skills, contacts, and personality traits to the point of lying, demands* to be recognized as superior without commensurate achievements);
- Is *obsessed* with fantasies of unlimited success, *fame, fearsome* power or *omnipotence, unequalled* brilliance (*the Cerebral Narcissist*), *bodily* beauty *or sexual performance* (*the Somatic Narcissist*), or ideal, *everlasting, all-conquering* love *or passion*;
- Firmly convinced that he or she is unique and, being special, can only be understood by, *should only be treated by*, or associate with, other special or unique, or high-status people (or institutions);
- Requires excessive admiration, *adulation, attention and affirmation, or, failing that, wishes to be feared and to be notorious (Narcissistic Supply)*;
- Feels entitled. *Demands automatic and full compliance* with his or her unreasonable expectations for special and *favourable, priority* treatment;
- Is "interpersonally exploitative", i.e., *uses* others to achieve his or her own ends;
- *Devoid* of empathy. Is *unable* or unwilling to identify with, *acknowledge, or accept* the feelings, needs, *preferences, wishes, priorities, and choices* of others;
- Constantly envious of others *and seeks to hurt or destroy the objects of his envy or the sources of her frustration. Suffers from persecutory (paranoid) delusions as he or she* believes that they feel the same about him or her *and are likely to act in the same destructive manner*;
- Behaves arrogantly and haughtily. *Feels superior, contemptuous, omnipotent, omniscient, invincible, immune,*

"above the law", and omnipresent (magical thinking). Rages when frustrated, contradicted, or confronted by people he or she considers inferior to him or her and unworthy.

[Click here to download a bibliography of the studies and research regarding Narcissistic Personality Disorder (NPD) on which I based my proposed revisions.]

Prevalence and Age and Gender Features

We are all narcissists to some degree. But healthy narcissism is adaptive, flexible, empathic, causes elation and joy (happiness), and helps us to function. Pathological narcissism is maladaptive, rigid, persisting, and causes significant distress, and functional impairment.

According to the DSM IV-TR, between 2% and 16% of the population in clinical settings (between 0.5-1% of the general population) are diagnosed with Narcissistic Personality Disorder (NPD). Most narcissists (50-75%, according to the DSM V) are men. The DSM V suggests that *"between 0% and 6.2% of community samples"* may be diagnosed with Narcissistic Personality Disorder based on the DSM IV criteria.

[See also: Psychotherapeutic Assessment and Treatment of Narcissistic Personality Disorder by Robert C. Schwartz, Ph.D., DAPA and Shannon D. Smith, Ph.D., DAPA (American Psychotherapy Association, Article 3004 Annals July/August 2002)]

We must carefully distinguish the narcissistic traits of adolescents – narcissism is an integral part of their healthy personal development – from the full-fledged disorder. Adolescence is about self-definition, differentiation, separation from one's parents, and individuation. These inevitably involve narcissistic assertiveness which is not to be conflated or confused with Narcissistic Personality Disorder (NPD).

Narcissistic Personality Disorder (NPD) is exacerbated by the onset of aging and the physical, mental, and occupational restrictions it imposes.

In certain situations, such as under constant public scrutiny and exposure, a transient and reactive form of Narcissistic Personality Disorder (NPD) has been observed by Robert Milman and labelled "Acquired Situational Narcissism".

There is only scant research regarding Narcissistic Personality Disorder (NPD), but studies did not demonstrate any cultural, social, ethnic, genetic, economic, or professional predilection to pathological narcissism.

Comorbidity and Differential Diagnoses

Narcissistic Personality Disorder (NPD) is often diagnosed with other mental health disorders ("comorbidity"), such as eating disorders, mood disorders, and substance-related disorders. Patients with Narcissistic Personality Disorder (NPD) are frequently abusive and prone to impulsive and reckless behaviours ("dual diagnosis").

Narcissistic Personality Disorder (NPD) is also commonly diagnosed with other personality disorders, such as Histrionic, Borderline, Paranoid, and Antisocial Personality Disorder.

The personal style of people who are afflicted with Narcissistic Personality Disorder (NPD) should be distinguished from the personal styles of patients with other Cluster B personality disorders. The narcissist is grandiose, the histrionic coquettish, the antisocial (psychopath) callous, and the borderline needy.

As opposed to patients with Borderline Personality Disorder, the self-image of the narcissist is stable, he or she is less impulsive and less self-defeating or self-destructive and less concerned with abandonment issues (not as clinging, labile, and erratic as the borderline).

Contrary to the histrionic patient, the narcissist is goal-orientated and proud of his or her possessions and accomplishments. Narcissists also rarely display their emotions as histrionics do and they hold the sensitivities and needs of others in contempt.

According to the DSM IV-TR both narcissists and psychopaths are *"tough-minded, glib, superficial, exploitative, and un-empathic"*. But narcissists are less impulsive, less aggressive, and less deceitful. Psychopaths rarely seek Narcissistic Supply (attention and adulation). As opposed to psychopaths, few narcissists are career criminals.

Patients with obsessive-compulsive disorders are committed to perfection and believe that only they are capable of attaining it. But, as opposed to narcissists, they are self-critical and far more aware of their own deficiencies, flaws, and shortcomings.

Clinical Features of Narcissistic Personality Disorder (NPD)

The onset of pathological narcissism is in infancy, childhood and early adolescence. It is commonly attributed to childhood abuse and trauma inflicted by parents, authority figures, or even peers. Pathological narcissism is largely a defence mechanism intended to deflect hurt and trauma from the victim's "True Self" into a

"False Self" which is construed by the narcissist to be omnipotent, invulnerable, and omniscient. The narcissist uses the False Self to regulate his or her labile sense of self-worth by extracting from his environment Narcissistic Supply (any form of attention, both positive and negative).

There is a whole range of narcissistic reactions, styles, and personalities: from the mild, reactive and transient to the permanent personality disorder.

Patients diagnosed with Narcissistic Personality Disorder (NPD) feel injured, humiliated, and empty when criticized. They often react with disdain (devaluation), rage, and defiance to any slight, real or imagined. To avoid such situations, some patients with Narcissistic Personality Disorder (NPD) socially withdraw and feign false modesty and humility to mask their underlying grandiosity. Dysthymic and depressive disorders are common reactions to isolation and feelings of shame and inadequacy.

The interpersonal relationships of patients with Narcissistic Personality Disorder are typically impaired owing to their lack of empathy, disregard for others, exploitativeness, sense of entitlement, and constant need for attention (Narcissistic Supply).

Though often ambitious, intelligent, and capable, inability to tolerate setbacks, disagreement, and criticism make it difficult for patients with Narcissistic Personality Disorder to work in a team or to maintain long-term professional achievements. The narcissist's fantastic grandiosity, frequently coupled with a hypomanic mood, is typically incommensurate with his or her real accomplishments (the "Grandiosity Gap").

Patients diagnosed with Narcissistic Personality Disorder are either "Cerebral" (derive their Narcissistic Supply from their intellect, or academic achievements), or "Somatic" (derive their Narcissistic Supply from their physique, exercise, physical or sexual prowess, and romantic or physical "conquests").

Patients with Narcissistic Personality Disorder are either "classic" (meet five of the nine diagnostic criteria included in the DSM), or they are "compensatory" (their narcissism compensates for deep-set feelings of inferiority and lack of self-worth).

Some narcissists are covert, or Inverted Narcissists. As codependents, they derive their Narcissistic Supply from their relationships with classic narcissists.

Based on a survey of 1201 therapists and psychologists in clinical practice, Prof. Drew Westen of Emory University postulated the existence of three subtypes of narcissists:

1. High functioning or Exhibitionist: *"(H)as an exaggerated sense of self-importance, but is also articulate, energetic, outgoing, and achievement oriented."* (The equivalent of the Cerebral Narcissist.)
2. Fragile: *"(W)ants to feel important and privileged to ward off painful feelings of inadequacy and loneliness."* (The equivalent of the compensatory narcissist.)
3. Grandiose or Malignant: *"(H)as an exaggerated sense of self-importance, feels privileged, exploits others, and lusts after power."* (The equivalent of the classic narcissist.)

[Westen, Drew et al. Refining the Construct of Narcissistic Personality Disorder: Diagnostic Criteria and Subtypes (Posted at http://ajp.psychiatryonline.org/pap.dtl)]

Treatment and Prognosis

The common treatment for patients with Narcissistic Personality Disorder (NPD) is talk therapy (mainly psychodynamic psychotherapy or cognitive-behavioural treatment modalities). Talk therapy is used to modify the narcissist's antisocial, interpersonally exploitative, and dysfunctional behaviours, often with some success. Medication is prescribed to control and ameliorate attendant conditions such as obsessive-compulsive disorders, or mood disorders.

The prognosis for an adult suffering from Narcissistic Personality Disorder (NPD) is poor, though his adaptation to life and to others can improve with treatment.

Narcissistic Personality Disorder in the DSM V

The DSM V re-defines personality disorders thus:

"The essential features of a personality disorder are impairments in personality (self and interpersonal) functioning and the presence of pathological personality traits."

According to the Alternative DSM V Model for Personality Disorders [p.767], the following criteria must be met to diagnose Narcissistic Personality Disorder (in parentheses my comments):

"Moderate or greater impairment in personality functioning in either identity, or self-direction (should be: in both).*"*

Identity

The narcissist keeps referring to others excessively in order to regulate his self-esteem (really, his sense of self-worth) and for his "self-definition" (to define his identity). His self-appraisal is exaggerated, whether it is inflated, deflated, or even fluctuating between these two poles and his emotional regulation reflects these vacillations.

(Finally, the DSM V accepted that narcissists can have an "inferiority complex" and feel worthless and bad; that they go through cycles of ups and downs in their self-evaluation; and that this cycling influences their mood and affect.)

Self-direction

The narcissist sets goals in order to gain approval from others (Narcissistic Supply; the DSM V ignores the fact that the run-of-the-mill narcissist finds disapproval equally rewarding as long as it places him firmly in the limelight). The narcissist lacks self-awareness as far as his motivation goes (and as far as everything else besides).

The narcissist's personal standards and benchmarks are either too high (which supports his grandiosity), or too low (buttresses his sense of entitlement, which is incommensurate with his real-life performance).

Impairments in interpersonal functioning in either empathy or intimacy (should be: in both).

Empathy

The narcissist finds it difficult to identify with the emotions and needs of others, but is very attuned to their reactions when they are relevant to himself (cold empathy). Consequently, he overestimates the effect he has on others or underestimates it (the classic narcissist never underestimates the effect he has on others - but the Inverted Narcissist does).

Intimacy

The narcissist's relationships are self-serving and, by implication, shallow and superficial. They are centred around and geared at the regulation of his self-esteem (obtaining Narcissistic Supply for the regulation of his labile sense of self-worth).

The narcissist is not "genuinely" interested in intimate experiences of his partner (implying that he does fake such interest convincingly). The narcissist emphasizes his need for personal gain (by using the word "need", the DSM V acknowledges the compulsive and addictive nature of Narcissistic Supply). These twin fixtures of the narcissist's relationships render them one-sided: no mutuality or reciprocity (no intimacy).

Pathological Personality Traits

Antagonism characterized by grandiosity and attention-seeking.

Grandiosity

Reference is made to the aforementioned feeling of entitlement. The DSM V adds that it can be either overt or covert (which corresponds to my taxonomy of classic and Inverted Narcissist).

Grandiosity is characterized by self-centredness; a firmly-held conviction of superiority (arrogance or haughtiness); and condescending or patronizing attitudes.

Attention-seeking

The narcissist puts inordinate effort, time, and resources into attracting others (Sources of Narcissistic Supply) and placing himself at the focus and centre of attention. He seeks admiration (the DSM V gets it completely wrong here: the narcissist does prefer to be admired and adulated, but, failing that, any kind of attention would do, even if it is negative).

The diagnostic criteria end with disclaimers and differential diagnoses, which, in turn, reflect years of accumulated research and newly-gained knowledge:

The above enumerated impairments should be *"stable across time and consistent across situations ... not better understood as normative for the individual's developmental stage or socio-cultural environment ... are not solely due to the direct physiological effects of a substance (e.g., a drug of abuse, medication) or a general medical condition (e.g., severe head trauma)."*

Psychological Defence Mechanisms

According to Freud and his followers, our psyche is a battlefield between instinctual urges and drives (the id), the constraints imposed by reality on the gratification of these impulses (the ego), and the norms of society (the superego). This constant infighting generates what Freud called "neurotic anxiety" (fear of losing control) and "moral anxiety" (guilt and shame).

But these are not the only types of anxiety. "Reality anxiety" is the fear of genuine threats and it combines with the other two to yield a morbid and surrealistic inner world.

These multiple, recurrent, "mini-panics" (combo anxieties) are potentially intolerable, overwhelming, and destructive – hence the need to defend against them. There are dozens of defence mechanisms. An overview of the most common follows:

Acting Out

When an inner conflict (most often, frustration) translates into aggression. It involves acting with little or no insight or reflection and in order to attract attention and disrupt other people's cozy lives.

Denial

Perhaps the most primitive and best known defence mechanism. People simply ignore unpleasant facts, they filter out data and content that contravene their self-image, prejudices, and preconceived notions of others and of the world.

Devaluation

Attributing negative or inferior traits or qualifiers to self or others. This is done in order to punish the person devalued and to mitigate his or her impact on and importance to the devaluer. When the self is devalued, it is a self-defeating and self-destructive act.

Displacement

When we cannot confront the real sources of our frustration, pain, and envy, we tend to pick a fight with someone weaker or irrelevant and, thus, less menacing. Children often do it because they perceive conflicts with parents and caregivers as life-threatening. Instead, they go out and torment the cat or bully someone at school or lash out at their siblings.

Dissociation

Our mental existence is continuous. We maintain a seamless flow of memories, consciousness, perception, and representation of both inner and external worlds. When we face horrors and unbearable truths, we sometimes "disengage". We lose track of space, time, and the continuum of our identity. We become "someone else" with minimal awareness of our surroundings, of incoming information, and of circumstances. In extreme cases, some people develop a permanently rent personality and this is known as Dissociative Identity Disorder (DID).

Fantasy

Everyone fantasizes now and then. It helps to fend off the dreariness and drabness of everyday life and to plan for an uncertain future. But when fantasy becomes a central feature of grappling with conflict, it is pathological. Seeking gratification – the satisfaction of drives or desires – mainly by fantasizing is an unhealthy defence. Narcissists, for instance, often indulge in grandiose fantasies which are incommensurate with their accomplishments and abilities. Such fantasy life retards personal growth and development because it substitutes for true coping.

Idealization

Another defence mechanism in the arsenal of the narcissist (and, to lesser degree, the borderline and histrionic) is the attribution of positive, glowing, and superior traits to self and (more commonly) to others. Again, what differentiates the healthy from the pathological is the reality test. Imputing positive characteristics to self or others is good, but only if the attributed qualities are real and grounded in a firm grasp of what's true and what's not.

Isolation of Affect

Cognition (thoughts, concepts, ideas) is never divorced from emotion. Conflict can be avoided by separating the cognitive content (for instance, a disturbing or depressing idea) from its emotional correlate. The subject is fully aware of the facts or of the intellectual dimensions of a problematic situation but feels numb. Casting away threatening and discomfiting feelings is a potent way of coping with conflict in the short-term. It is only when it become habitual that it rendered self-defeating.

Omnipotence

When one has a pervading sense and image of oneself as incredibly powerful, superior, irresistible, intelligent, or influential. This is not an adopted affectation but an ingrained, ineradicable inner conviction which borders on magical thinking. It is intended to fend off expected hurt in having to acknowledge one's shortcomings, inadequacies, or limitations.

Projection

We all have an image of how we "should be". Freud called it the "ego ideal". But sometimes we experience emotions and drives or have personal qualities which don't sit well with this idealized construct. Projection is when we attribute to others these unacceptable, discomfiting, and ill-fitting feelings and traits that we possess. This way we disown these discordant features and secure the right to criticize and chastise others for having or displaying them. When entire collectives (nations, groups, organizations, firms) project, Freud calls it the "narcissism of small differences."

Projective Identification

Projection is unconscious. People are rarely aware that they are projecting onto others their own ego-dystonic and unpleasant characteristics and feelings. But, sometimes, the content thus projected is retained in the subject's awareness. This creates a conflict. On the one hand, the patient cannot admit that the emotions, traits, reactions, and behaviours that he so condemns in others are really his. On the other hand, he can't help but being self-aware. He fails to erase from his consciousness the painful realization that he is merely projecting.

So, instead of denying it, the subject explains unpleasant emotions and unacceptable conduct as reactions to the recipient's behaviour. "She made me do it!" is the battle cry of Projective Identification.

We all have expectations regarding the world and its denizens. Some people expect to be loved and appreciated – others to be feared and abused. The latter behave obnoxiously and thus force their nearest and dearest to hate, fear, and "abuse" them. Thus vindicated, their expectations fulfilled, they calm down. The world is rendered once more familiar by making other people behave the way they expect them to. "I knew you would cheat on me! It was clear I couldn't trust you!"

Rationalization or Intellectualization

To cast one's behaviour after the fact in a favourable light. To justify and explain one's conduct or, more often, misconduct by resorting to "rational, logical, socially-acceptable" explications and excuses. Rationalization is also used to re-establish ego-syntony (inner peace and self-acceptance).

Though not strictly a defence mechanism, cognitive dissonance may be considered a variant of rationalization. It involves speech acts which amount to the devaluation of things and people very much desired but frustratingly out of one's reach and control. In a famous fable, a fox, unable to snag the luscious grapes he covets, says: "These grapes are probably sour anyhow!" This is an example of cognitive dissonance in action.

Reaction Formation

Adopting a position and mode of conduct that defy personally unacceptable thoughts or impulses by expressing diametrically opposed sentiments and convictions. Example: a latent (closet) homosexual finds his sexual preference deplorable and acutely shameful (ego-dystonic). He resorts to homophobia. He publicly berates, taunts, and baits homosexuals. Additionally, he may flaunt his heterosexuality by emphasizing his sexual prowess, or by prowling singles bars for easy pick-ups and conquests. This way he contains and avoids his unwelcome homosexuality.

Repression

The removal from consciousness of forbidden thoughts and wishes. The removed content does not vanish and it remains as potent as ever, fermenting in one's unconscious. It is liable to create inner conflicts and anxiety and provoke other defence mechanisms to cope with these.

Splitting

This is a "primitive" defence mechanism. In other words, it begins to operate in very early infancy. It involves the inability to integrate contradictory qualities of the same object into a coherent picture. Mother has good qualities and bad, sometimes she is attentive and caring and sometimes distracted and cold. The baby is unable to grasp the complexities of her personality. Instead, the infant invents two constructs (entities), "Bad Mother" and "Good Mother". It relegates everything likable about mother to the "Good Mother" and contrasts it with "Bad Mother", the repository of everything it dislikes about her.

This means that whenever mother acts nicely, the baby relates to the idealized "Good Mother" and whenever mother fails the test, the baby devalues her by interacting, in its mind, with "Bad Mother". These cycles of idealization followed by devaluation are common in some personality disorders, notably Narcissistic and Borderline.

Splitting can also apply to one's self. Patients with personality disorders often idealize themselves fantastically and grandiosely, only to harshly devalue, hate, and even harm themselves when they fail or are otherwise frustrated.

Sublimation

The conversion and channelling of unacceptable emotions into socially-condoned behaviour. Freud described how sexual desires and urges are transformed into creative pursuits or politics.

Undoing

Trying to rid oneself of gnawing feelings of guilt by compensating the injured party either symbolically or actually.

Return

The Narcissist's Entitlement of Routine

I hate routine. When I find myself doing the same things over and over again, I get depressed. I oversleep, over-eat, over-drink and, in general, engage in addictive, impulsive and compulsive behaviours. This is my way of re-introducing risk and excitement into what I (emotionally) perceive to be a barren life.

The problem is that even the most exciting and varied existence becomes routine after a while. Living in the same country or apartment, meeting the same people, doing essentially the same things (though with changing content) – all "qualify" as stultifying rote.

I feel entitled to more. I feel it is my right – due to my intellectual superiority – to lead a thrilling, rewarding, kaleidoscopic life. I feel entitled to force life itself, or, at least, people around me – to yield to my wishes and needs, supreme among them the need for stimulating variety.

This rejection of habit is part of a larger pattern of aggressive entitlement. I feel that the very existence of a sublime intellect (such as myself) warrants concessions and allowances. Standing in line is a waste of time best spent pursuing knowledge, inventing and creating. I should avail myself of the best medical treatment proffered by the most prominent medical authorities – lest the asset that is I be lost to Mankind. I should not be bothered with proofreading my articles (or even re-reading them) – these lowly jobs best be assigned to the less gifted. The devil is in paying precious attention to details.

Entitlement is sometimes justified in a Picasso or an Einstein. But I am neither. My achievements are grotesquely incommensurate with my overwhelming sense of entitlement. I am but a mediocre and forgettable scribbler who, at the age of 39, is a colossal under-achiever, if anything.

Of course, the feeling of supremacy often serves to mask a cancerous complex of inferiority. Moreover, I infect others with my projected grandiosity and their feedback constitutes the edifice upon which I construct my self-esteem. I regulate my sense of self-worth by rigidly insisting that I am above the madding crowd while deriving my Narcissistic Supply from this very thus despised source.

But there is a second angle to this abhorrence of the predictable. As a narcissist, I employ a host of Emotional Involvement Prevention Mechanisms (EIPM). Despising routine and avoiding it is one of these mechanisms. Their function is to prevent me from getting emotionally involved and, subsequently, hurt. Their application results in an "approach-avoidance repetition complex". The narcissist, fearing and loathing intimacy, stability and security – yet craving them – approaches and then avoids significant others or important tasks in a rapid succession of apparently inconsistent and disconnected behaviours.

Negativistic (Passive-Aggressive) Personality Disorder

Negativistic (Passive-Aggressive) Personality Disorder is not yet recognized by the DSM Committee. It makes its appearances in Appendix B of the Diagnostic and Statistical Manual, titled "Criteria Sets and Axes Provided for Further Study".

Some people are perennial pessimists and harbour "negative energy" and negativistic attitudes ("good things don't last", "it doesn't pay to be good", "the future is behind me"). Not only do they disparage the efforts of others, but they make it a point to resist demands to perform in workplace and social settings and to frustrate people's expectations and requests, however reasonable and minimal they may be. Such persons regard every requirement and assigned task as impositions, reject authority, resent authority figures (boss, teacher, parent-like spouse), feel shackled and enslaved by commitment, and oppose relationships that bind them in any manner.

Whether these attitudes and behaviours are acquired/learned or the outcome of heredity is still an open question. Often, passive-aggression is the only weapon of the weak and the meek, besieged as they are by frustration, helplessness, envy and spite, the organizing principles of their emotional landscape and the engines and main motivating forces of their lives.

Passive-aggressiveness wears a multitude of guises: malingering, procrastination, perfectionism, neglect, truancy, intentional inefficiency, forgetfulness, stubbornness, and outright sabotage.

This repeated and advertent misconduct has far reaching effects. Consider the Negativist in the workplace: he or she invests time and efforts in obstructing his or her own chores and in undermining relationships. But, these self-destructive and self-defeating behaviours wreak havoc throughout the workshop, or the office.

People who are diagnosed with Negativistic (Passive-Aggressive) Personality Disorder resemble narcissists in important respects. Despite the obstructive role they play, passive-aggressives feel unappreciated, underpaid, cheated, and misunderstood. They chronically complain, whine, carp, and criticize. They blame their failures and defeats on others, posing as martyrs and victims of a corrupt, inefficient, and heartless system (in other words, they have alloplastic defences and an external locus of control).

Passive-aggressives sulk and give others the "silent treatment" in reaction to real or imagined slights. They suffer from ideas and delusions of reference (i.e. they believe that they are the butt of derision, contempt, and condemnation) and are mildly paranoid (the world is out to get them, which accounts for their personal misfortunes).

In the words of the DSM:

"They may be sullen, irritable, impatient, argumentative, cynical, sceptical and contrary." They are also hostile, explosive, lack impulse control, and, sometimes, reckless.

Inevitably, passive-aggressives are envious of the fortunate, the successful, the famous, the happy, their superiors, and those in favour. Whenever given the opportunity, they vent this venomous jealousy openly, virulently, and defiantly. But, deep at heart, passive-aggressives are inordinately craven. When reprimanded, they immediately revert to begging forgiveness, kowtowing, or maudlin protestations, turning on their charm, and promising to behave and perform better in the future.

Passive-aggressive Bureaucracies

Collectives – especially bureaucracies, such as for-profit universities, health maintenance organizations (HMOs), the government, and army – tend to behave passive-aggressively and to frustrate their constituencies. This misconduct is often aimed at releasing tensions and stress that the officials (individuals) comprising these organizations accumulate in their daily contact with members of the public.

Additionally, as Kafka astutely observed, such misbehaviour fosters dependence in the clients of these establishments and cements a relationship of superior (i.e., the obstructionist group) versus inferior (the demanding and deserving individual, who is reduced to begging and supplicating).

Passive-aggressiveness has a lot in common with pathological narcissism: the destructive envy; the recurrent attempts to buttress grandiose fantasies of omnipotence and omniscience; the lack of impulse control; the deficient ability to empathize; and the sense of entitlement, often incommensurate with real-life achievements.

No wonder, therefore, that negativistic, narcissistic, and borderline organizations share similar traits and identical psychological defences: most notably denial (mainly of the existence of problems and complaints), and projection (blaming the group's failures and dysfunction on its clients).

In such a state of mind, it is easy to confuse means (making money, hiring staff, constructing or renting facilities, and so on) with ends (providing loans, educating students, assisting the poor, fighting wars, etc.). Means become ends and ends become means.

Consequently, the original goals of such organizations are now considered to be nothing more than obstacles on the way to realizing new aims: borrowers, students, or the poor are nuisances to be summarily dispensed with as the board of directors considers the erection of yet another office tower and the disbursement of yet another annual bonus to its members. As Parkinson noted, the collective perpetuates its existence, regardless of whether it has any role left and how well it functions.

As the constituencies of these collectives – most forcefully, its clients – protest and exert pressure in an attempt to restore them to their erstwhile state, the collectives develop a paranoid state of mind, a siege mentality, replete with persecutory delusions and aggressive behaviour. This anxiety is an introjection of guilt. Deep inside, these organizations know that they have strayed from the right path. They anticipate attacks and rebukes and are rendered defensive, paranoid, and suspicious by the inevitable, impending onslaught.

Still, deep down bureaucracies epitomize the predominant culture of failure: failure as a product, the intended outcome and end-result of complex, deliberate, and arduous manufacturing processes. Like the majority of people, bureaucrats are emotionally invested in failure, not in success: they thrive on failure, calamity, and emergency. The worse the disaster and inaptitude, the more resources are allocated to voracious and ever-expanding bureaucracies (think the US government post the

9/11 terrorist attacks). Paradoxically, their measure of success is in how many failures they have had to endure or have fostered.

These massive organs tend to attract and nurture functionaries and clients whose mentality and personality are suited to embedded fatalism. In a globalized, competitive world the majority are doomed to failure and recurrent deprivation. Those rendered losers by the vagaries and exigencies of modernity find refuge in Leviathan: imposing, metastatically sprawling nanny organizations and corporations who shield them from the agonizing truth of their own inadequacy and from the shearing winds of entrepreneurship and cutthroat struggle.

A tiny minority of mavericks swim against this inexorable tide: they innovate, reframe, invent, and lead. Theirs is an existence of constant strife as the multitudes and their weaponized bureaucracies seek to put them down, to extinguish the barely flickering flame, and to appropriate the scant resources consumed by these forward leaps. In time, ironically, truly successful entrepreneurs themselves become invested in failure and form their own vast establishment empires: defensive and dedicated rather than open and universal networks. Progress materializes despite and in contradistinction to the herd-like human spirit - not because of it.

Return

Pathological Narcissism
A Dysfunction or a Blessing?

Comments on recent research by Roy Baumeister.

Is pathological narcissism a blessing or a malediction?

The answer is: it depends. Healthy narcissism is a mature, balanced love of oneself coupled with a stable sense of self-worth and self-esteem. Healthy narcissism implies knowledge of one's boundaries and a proportionate and realistic appraisal of one's achievements and traits.

Pathological narcissism is wrongly described as too much healthy narcissism (or too much self-esteem). These are two absolutely unrelated phenomena which, regrettably, came to bear the same title. Confusing pathological narcissism with self-esteem betrays a fundamental ignorance of both.

Pathological narcissism involves an impaired, dysfunctional, immature (True) Self coupled with a compensatory fiction (the False Self). The sick narcissist's sense of self-worth and self-esteem derive entirely from audience feedback. The narcissist has no self-esteem or self-worth of his own (no such ego functions). In the absence of observers, the narcissist shrivels to non-existence and feels dead. Hence the narcissist's preying habits in his constant pursuit of Narcissistic Supply. Pathological narcissism is an addictive behaviour.

Still, dysfunctions are reactions to abnormal environments and situations (e.g., abuse, trauma, smothering, etc.).

Paradoxically, his dysfunction allows the narcissist to function. It compensates for lacks and deficiencies by exaggerating tendencies and traits. It is like the tactile sense of a blind person. In short: pathological narcissism is a result of over-sensitivity, the repression of overwhelming memories and experiences, and the suppression of inordinately strong negative feelings (e.g., hurt, envy, anger, or humiliation).

That the narcissist functions at all – is because of his pathology and thanks to it. The alternative is complete decompensation and integration.

In time, the narcissist learns how to leverage his pathology, how to use it to his advantage, how to deploy it in order to maximise benefits and utilities – in other words, how to transform his curse into a blessing.

Narcissists are obsessed by delusions of fantastic grandeur and superiority. As a result they are very competitive. They are strongly compelled – where others are merely motivated. They are driven, relentless, tireless, and ruthless. They often make it to the top. But even when they do not – they strive and fight and learn and climb and create and think and devise and design and conspire. Faced with a challenge – they are likely to do better than non-narcissists.

Yet, we often find that narcissists abandon their efforts in mid-stream, give up, vanish, lose interest, devalue former pursuits, or slump. Why is that?

Narcissists are prone to self-defeating and self-destructive behaviours.

The Self-Punishing, Guilt-Purging Behaviours

These are intended to inflict punishment on the narcissist and thus instantly relieve him of his overwhelming anxiety.

This is very reminiscent of a compulsive-ritualistic behaviour. The narcissist feels guilty. It could be an "ancient" guilt, a "sexual" guilt (Freud), or a "social" guilt. In early life, the narcissist internalised and introjected the voices of meaningful and authoritative others – parents, role models, peers – that consistently and convincingly judged him to be no good, blameworthy, deserving of punishment or retaliation, or corrupt.

First published on the Suite 101 Narcissistic Personality Disorders Topic.

Return

The Narcissist's Confabulated Life

Confabulations are an important part of life. They serve to heal emotional wounds or to prevent ones from being inflicted in the first place. They prop-up the confabulator's self-esteem, regulate his (or her) sense of self-worth, and buttress his (or her) self-image. They serve as organising principles in social interactions.

Father's wartime heroism, mother's youthful good looks, one's oft-recounted exploits, erstwhile alleged brilliance, and past purported sexual irresistibility – are typical examples of white, fuzzy, heart-warming lies wrapped around a shrivelled kernel of truth.

But the distinction between reality and fantasy is rarely completely lost. Deep inside, the healthy confabulator knows where facts end and wishful thinking takes over. Father acknowledges he was no war hero, though he did his share of fighting. Mother understands she was no ravishing beauty, though she may have been attractive. The confabulator realises that his recounted exploits are overblown, his brilliance exaggerated, and his sexual irresistibility a myth.

Such distinctions never rise to the surface because everyone – the confabulator and his audience alike – have a common interest to maintain the confabulation. To challenge the integrity of the confabulator or the veracity of his confabulations is to threaten the very fabric of family and society. Human intercourse is built around such entertaining deviations from the truth.

This is where the narcissist differs from others (from "normal" people).

His very self is a piece of fiction concocted to fend off hurt and to nurture the narcissist's grandiosity. He fails in his "reality test" – the ability to distinguish the actual from the imagined. The narcissist fervently believes in his own infallibility, brilliance, omnipotence, heroism, and perfection. He doesn't dare confront the truth and admit it even to himself.

Moreover, he imposes his personal mythology on his nearest and dearest. Spouse, children, colleagues, friends, neighbours – sometimes even perfect strangers – must abide by the narcissist's narrative or face his wrath. The narcissist countenances no disagreement, alternative points of view, or criticism. To him, confabulation IS reality.

The coherence of the narcissist's dysfunctional and precariously-balanced personality depends on the plausibility of his stories and on their acceptance by his Sources of Narcissistic Supply. The narcissist invests an inordinate time in substantiating his tales, collecting "evidence", defending his version of events, and in re-interpreting reality to fit his scenario. As a result, most narcissists are self-delusional, obstinate, opinionated, and argumentative.

The narcissist's lies are not goal-orientated. This is what makes his constant dishonesty both disconcerting and incomprehensible. The narcissist lies at the drop of a hat, needlessly, and almost ceaselessly. He lies in order to avoid the Grandiosity Gap – when the abyss between fact and (narcissistic) fiction becomes too gaping to ignore.

The narcissist lies in order to preserve appearances, uphold fantasies, support the tall (and impossible) tales of his False Self and extract Narcissistic Supply from unsuspecting sources, who are not yet on to him. To the narcissist, confabulation is not merely a way of life – but life itself.

We are all conditioned to let other indulge in pet delusions and get away with white, not too egregious, lies. The narcissist makes use of our socialisation. We dare not confront or expose him, despite the outlandishness of his claims, the improbability of his stories, the implausibility of his alleged accomplishments and conquests. We simply turn the other cheek, or meekly avert our eyes, often embarrassed.

Moreover, the narcissist makes clear, from the very beginning, that it is his way or the highway. His aggression – even violent streak – are close to the surface. He may be charming in a first encounter – but even then there are telltale signs of pent-up abuse. His interlocutors sense this impending threat and avoid conflict by acquiescing with the narcissist's fairy tales. Thus he imposes his private universe and virtual reality on his milieu – sometimes with disastrous consequences.

Return

The Cult of the Narcissist

The narcissist is the guru at the centre of a cult. Like other gurus, he demands complete obedience from his flock: his spouse, his offspring, other family members, friends, and colleagues. He feels entitled to adulation and special treatment by his followers. He punishes the wayward and the straying lambs. He enforces discipline, adherence to his teachings, and common goals. The less accomplished he is in reality – the more stringent his mastery and the more pervasive the brainwashing.

The – often involuntary – members of the narcissist's mini-cult inhabit a twilight zone of his own construction. He imposes on them a shared psychosis, replete with persecutory delusions, "enemies", mythical narratives, and apocalyptic scenarios if he is flouted.

The narcissist's control is based on ambiguity, unpredictability, fuzziness, and ambient abuse. His ever-shifting whims exclusively define right versus wrong, desirable and unwanted, what is to be pursued and what to be avoided. He alone determines the rights and obligations of his disciples and alters them at will.

The narcissist is a micro-manager. He exerts control over the minutest details and behaviours. He punishes severely and abuses withholders of information and those who fail to conform to his wishes and goals.

The narcissist does not respect the boundaries and privacy of his reluctant adherents. He ignores their wishes and treats them as objects or instruments of gratification. He seeks to control both situations and people compulsively.

He strongly disapproves of others' personal autonomy and independence. Even innocuous activities, such as meeting a friend or visiting one's family require his permission. Gradually, he isolates his nearest and dearest until they are fully dependent on him emotionally, sexually, financially, and socially.

He acts in a patronising and condescending manner and criticises often. He alternates between emphasising the minutest faults (devalues) and exaggerating the talents, traits, and skills (idealises) of the members of his cult. He is wildly unrealistic in his expectations – which legitimises his subsequent abusive conduct.

The narcissist claims to be infallible, superior, talented, skilful, omnipotent, and omniscient. He often lies and confabulates to support these unfounded claims. Within his cult, he expects awe, admiration, adulation, and constant attention commensurate with his outlandish stories and assertions. He reinterprets reality to fit his fantasies.

His thinking is dogmatic, rigid, and doctrinaire. He does not countenance free thought, pluralism, or free speech and doesn't brook criticism and disagreement. He demands – and often gets – complete trust and the relegation to his capable hands of all decision-making.

He forces the participants in his cult to be hostile to critics, the authorities, institutions, his personal enemies, or the media – if they try to uncover his actions and reveal the truth. He closely monitors and censors information from the outside, exposing his captive audience only to selective data and analyses.

The narcissist's cult is "missionary" and "imperialistic". He is always on the lookout for new recruits – his spouse's friends, his daughter's girlfriends, his neighbours, new colleagues at work. He immediately attempts to "convert" them to his "creed" – to convince them how wonderful and admirable he is. In other words, he tries to render them Sources of Narcissistic Supply.

Often, his behaviour on these "recruiting missions" is different to his conduct within the "cult". In the first phases of wooing new admirers and proselytising to potential "conscripts" – the narcissist is attentive, compassionate, empathic, flexible, self-effacing, and helpful. At home, among the "veterans" he is tyrannical, demanding, wilful, opinionated, aggressive, and exploitative.

As the leader of his congregation, the narcissist feels entitled to special amenities and benefits not accorded the "rank and file". He expects to be waited on hand and foot, to make free use of everyone's money and dispose of their assets liberally, and to be cynically exempt from the rules that he himself established (if such violation is pleasurable or gainful).

In extreme cases, the narcissist feels above the law - any kind of law. This grandiose and haughty conviction leads to criminal acts, incestuous or polygamous relationships, and recurrent friction with the authorities.

Hence the narcissist's panicky and sometimes violent reactions to "dropouts" from his cult. There's a lot going on that the narcissist wants kept under wraps. Moreover, the narcissist stabilises his fluctuating sense of self-worth by deriving Narcissistic Supply from his victims. Abandonment threatens the narcissist's precariously balanced personality.

Add to that the narcissist's paranoid and schizoid tendencies, his lack of introspective self-awareness, and his stunted sense of humour (lack of self-deprecation) and the risks to the grudging members of his cult are clear.

The narcissist sees enemies and conspiracies everywhere. He often casts himself as the heroic victim (martyr) of dark and stupendous forces. In every deviation from his tenets he espies malevolent and ominous subversion. He, therefore, is bent on disempowering his devotees. By any and all means.

The narcissist is dangerous.

Return

Bibliography

1. Alford, C. Fred. Narcissism: Socrates, the Frankfurt School and Psychoanalytic Theory. New Haven and London, Yale University Press, 1988
2. Devereux, George. Basic Problems of Ethno-Psychiatry. University of Chicago Press, 1980
3. Fairbairn, W. R. D. An Object Relations Theory of the Personality. New York, Basic Books, 1954
4. Freud S. Three Essays on the Theory of Sexuality [1905]. Standard Edition of the Complete Psychological Works of Sigmund Freud. Vol. 7. London, Hogarth Press, 1964
5. Freud, S. On Narcissism. Standard Ed. Vol. 14, pp. 73-107
6. Goldman, Howard H. (Ed.). Review of General Psychiatry. 4th Ed. London, Prentice Hall International, 1995
7. Golomb, Elan. Trapped in the Mirror: Adult Children of Narcissists in Their Struggle for Self. Quill, 1995
8. Greenberg, Jay R. and Mitchell, Stephen A. Object Relations in Psychoanalytic Theory. Cambridge, Mass., Harvard University Press, 1983
9. Grunberger, Bela. Narcissism: Psychoanalytic Essays. New York, International Universities Press, 1979
10. Guntrip, Harry. Personality Structure and Human Interaction. New York, International Universities Press, 1961
11. Horowitz M. J. Sliding Meanings: A Defence against Threat in Narcissistic Personalities. International Journal of Psychoanalytic Psychotherapy, 1975; 4:167
12. Horovitz M. J. Stress Response Syndromes: PTSD, Grief and Adjustment Disorders. 3rd Ed. New York, NY University Press, 1998
13. Jacobson, Edith. The Self and the Object World. New York, International Universities Press, 1964

14. Jung, C.G. Collected Works. G. Adler, M. Fordham and H. Read (Eds.). 21 volumes. Princeton University Press, 1960-1983
15. Kernberg O. Borderline Conditions and Pathological Narcissism. New York, Jason Aronson, 1975
16. Klein, Melanie. The Writings of Melanie Klein. Roger Money-Kyrle (Ed.). 4 Vols. New York, Free Press, 1964-75
17. Kohut H. The Chicago Institute Lectures 1972-1976. Marian and Paul Tolpin (Eds.). Analytic Press, 1998
18. Kohut M. The Analysis of the Self. New York, International Universities Press, 1971
19. Lasch, Christopher. The Culture of Narcissism. New York, Warner Books, 1979
20. Levine, J. D., and Weiss, Rona H. The Dynamics and Treatment of Alcoholism. Jason Aronson, 1994
21. Lowen, Alexander. Narcissism: Denial of the True Self. Touchstone Books, 1997
22. Millon, Theodore (and Roger D. Davis, contributor). Disorders of Personality: DSM-IV and Beyond. 2nd ed. New York, John Wiley and Sons, 1995
23. Millon, Theodore. Personality Disorders in Modern Life. New York, John Wiley and Sons, 2000
24. Riso, Don Richard. Personality Types: Using the Enneagram for Self-Discovery. Boston: Houghton Mifflin 1987
25. Roningstam, Elsa F. (Ed.). Disorders of Narcissism: Diagnostic, Clinical, and Empirical Implications. American Psychiatric Press, 1998
26. Rothstein, Arnold. The Narcissistic Pursuit of Reflection. 2nd revised Ed. New York, International Universities Press, 1984
27. Schwartz, Lester. Narcissistic Personality Disorders – A Clinical Discussion. Journal of American Psychoanalytic Association – 22 [1974]: 292-305
28. Salant-Schwartz, Nathan. Narcissism and Character Transformation. Inner City Books, 1985 – pp. 90-91
29. Stern, Daniel. The Interpersonal World of the Infant: A View from Psychoanalysis and Developmental Psychology. New York, Basic Books, 1985
30. Vaknin, Sam. Malignant Self Love – Narcissism Revisited. Skopje and Prague, Narcissus Publications, 2003
31. Zweig, Paul. The Heresy of Self Love: A Study of Subversive Individualism. New York, Basic Books, 1968

Return

The Narcissist And the Psychopath In the Workplace

The Narcissist in the Workplace

The Narcissist in the Workplace

To a narcissistic employer, the members of his "staff" are Secondary Sources of Narcissistic Supply. Their role is to accumulate the supply (remember events that support the grandiose self-image of the narcissist) and to regulate the Narcissistic Supply of the narcissist during dry spells – to adulate, adore, admire, agree, provide attention and approval, and, generally, serve as an audience to him.

The staff (or should we say "stuff"?) is supposed to remain passive. The narcissist is not interested in anything but the simplest function of mirroring. When the mirror acquires a personality and a life of its own, the narcissist is incensed. When independent minded, an employee might be in danger of being sacked by his narcissistic employer (an act which demonstrates the employer's omnipotence).

The employee's presumption to be the employer's equal by trying to befriend him (friendship is possible only among equals) injures the employer narcissistically. He is willing to accept his employees as underlings, whose very position serves to support his grandiose fantasies.

But his grandiosity is so tenuous and rests on such fragile foundations, that any hint of equality, disagreement or need (any intimation that the narcissist "needs" friends, for instance) threatens the narcissist profoundly. The narcissist is exceedingly insecure. It is easy to destabilise his impromptu "personality". His reactions are merely in self-defence.

Classic narcissistic behaviour is when idealisation is followed by devaluation. The devaluing attitude develops as a result of disagreements or simply because time has eroded the employee's capacity to serve as a FRESH Source of Supply.

The veteran employee, now taken for granted by his narcissistic employer, becomes uninspiring as a source of adulation, admiration and attention. The narcissist always seeks new thrills and stimuli.

The narcissist is notorious for his low threshold of resistance to boredom. His behaviour is impulsive and his biography tumultuous precisely because of his need to introduce uncertainty and risk to what he regards as "stagnation" or "slow death" (i.e., routine). Most interactions in the workplace are part of the rut – and thus constitute a reminder of this routine – deflating the narcissist's grandiose fantasies.

Narcissists do many unnecessary, wrong and even dangerous things in pursuit of the stabilisation of their inflated self-image.

Narcissists feel suffocated by intimacy, or by the constant reminders of the REAL, nitty-gritty world out there. It reduces them, makes them realise the Grandiosity Gap between their fantasies and reality. It is a threat to the precarious balance of their personality structures ("false" and invented) and treated by them as a menace.

Narcissists forever shift the blame, pass the buck, and engage in cognitive dissonance. They "pathologise" the other, foster feelings of guilt and shame in her, demean, debase and humiliate in order to preserve their sense of superiority.

Narcissists are pathological liars. They think nothing of it because their very Self is False, their own confabulation.

Here are a few useful guidelines:
- Never disagree with the narcissist or contradict him;
- Never offer him any intimacy;
- Look awed by whatever attribute matters to him (for instance: by his professional achievements or by his good looks, or by his success with women and so on);
- Never remind him of life out there and if you do, connect it somehow to his sense of grandiosity. You can aggrandise even your office supplies, the most mundane thing conceivable by saying: "These are the BEST art materials ANY workplace is going to have", "We get them EXCLUSIVELY", etc.;
- Do not make any comment, which might directly or indirectly impinge on the narcissist's self-image, omnipotence, superior judgement, omniscience, skills, capabilities, professional record, or even omnipresence. Bad sentences start with: "I think you overlooked ... made a mistake here ... you don't know ... do you know ... you were not here yesterday so ... you cannot ... you should ... (interpreted as rude imposition, narcissists

react very badly to perceived restrictions placed on their freedom) ... I (never mention the fact that you are a separate, independent entity, narcissists regard others as extensions of their selves)..." You get the gist of it.

Manage your narcissistic boss. Notice patterns in his bullying. Is he more aggressive on Monday mornings - and more open to suggestions on Friday afternoon? Is he amenable to flattery? Can you modify his conduct by appealing to his morality, superior knowledge, good manners, cosmopolitanism, or upbringing? Manipulating the narcissist is the only way to survive in such a tainted workplace.

Can the narcissist be harnessed? Can his energies be channelled productively?

This would be a deeply flawed - and even dangerous - "advice". Various management gurus purport to teach us how to harness this force of nature known as malignant or pathological narcissism. Narcissists are driven, visionary, ambitious, exciting and productive, says Michael Maccoby, for instance. To ignore such a resource is a criminal waste. All we need to do is learn how to "handle" them.

Yet, this prescription is either naive or disingenuous. Narcissists cannot be "handled", or "managed", or "contained", or "channelled". They are, by definition, incapable of team work. They lack empathy, are exploitative, envious, haughty and feel entitled, even if such a feeling is commensurate only with their grandiose fantasies and when their accomplishments are meagre.

Narcissists dissemble, conspire, destroy and self-destruct. Their drive is compulsive, their vision rarely grounded in reality, their human relations a calamity. In the long run, there is no enduring benefit to dancing with narcissists - only ephemeral and, often, fallacious, "achievements".

Return

Narcissism in the Boardroom

The perpetrators of the recent spate of financial frauds in the USA acted with callous disregard for both their employees and shareholders – not to mention other stakeholders. Psychologists have often remote-diagnosed them as "malignant, pathological narcissists".

Narcissists are driven by the need to uphold and maintain a False Self – a concocted, grandiose, and demanding psychological construct typical of the Narcissistic Personality Disorder. The False Self is projected to the world in order to garner Narcissistic Supply – adulation, admiration, or even notoriety and infamy. Any kind of attention is usually deemed by narcissists to be preferable to obscurity.

The False Self is suffused with fantasies of perfection, grandeur, brilliance, infallibility, immunity, significance, omnipotence, omnipresence, and omniscience. To be a narcissist is to be convinced of a great, inevitable personal destiny. The narcissist is preoccupied with ideal love, the construction of brilliant, revolutionary scientific theories, the composition or authoring or painting of the greatest work of art, the founding of a new school of thought, the attainment of fabulous wealth, the reshaping of a nation or a conglomerate, and so on. The narcissist never sets realistic goals to himself. He is forever preoccupied with fantasies of uniqueness, record breaking, or breathtaking achievements. His verbosity reflects this propensity.

Reality is, naturally, quite different and this gives rise to a Grandiosity Gap. The demands of the False Self are never satisfied by the narcissist's accomplishments, standing, wealth, clout, sexual prowess, or knowledge. The narcissist's grandiosity and sense of entitlement are equally incommensurate with his achievements.

To bridge the Grandiosity Gap, the malignant (pathological) narcissist resorts to shortcuts. These very often lead to fraud.

The narcissist cares only about appearances. What matters to him are the facade of wealth and its attendant social status and Narcissistic Supply. Witness the travestied extravagance of Tyco's Denis Kozlowski. Media attention only exacerbates the narcissist's addiction and makes it incumbent on him to go to ever-wilder extremes to secure uninterrupted supply from this source.

The narcissist lacks empathy – the ability to put himself in other people's shoes. He does not recognise boundaries – personal, corporate, or legal. Everything and everyone are to him mere instruments, extensions, objects unconditionally and uncomplainingly available in his pursuit of narcissistic gratification.

This makes the narcissist perniciously exploitative. He uses, abuses, devalues, and discards even his nearest and dearest in the most chilling manner. The narcissist is utility – driven, obsessed with his overwhelming need to reduce his anxiety and regulate his labile sense of self-worth by securing a constant supply of his drug – attention. American executives acted without compunction when they raided their employees' pension funds – as did Robert Maxwell a generation earlier in Britain.

The narcissist is convinced of his superiority – cerebral or physical. To his mind, he is a Gulliver hamstrung by a horde of narrow-minded and envious Lilliputians. The dotcom "new economy" was infested with "visionaries" with a contemptuous attitude towards the mundane: profits, business cycles, conservative economists, doubtful journalists, and cautious analysts.

Yet, deep inside, the narcissist is painfully aware of his addiction to others – their attention, admiration, applause, and affirmation. He despises himself for being thus dependent. He hates people the same way a drug addict hates his pusher. He wishes to "put them in their place", humiliate them, demonstrate to them how inadequate and imperfect they are in comparison to his regal self and how little he craves or needs them.

The narcissist regards himself as one would an expensive present, a gift to his company, to his family, to his neighbours, to his colleagues, to his country. This firm conviction of his inflated importance makes him feel entitled to special treatment, special favours, special outcomes, concessions, subservience, immediate gratification, obsequiousness, and lenience. It also makes him feel immune to mortal laws and somehow divinely protected and insulated from the inevitable consequences of his deeds and misdeeds.

The self-destructive narcissist plays the role of the "bad guy" (or "bad girl"). But even this is within the traditional social roles cartoonishly exaggerated by the narcissist to attract attention. Men are likely to emphasise intellect, power, aggression, money, or social status. Narcissistic women are likely to emphasise body, looks, charm, sexuality, feminine "traits", homemaking, children and childrearing.

Punishing the wayward narcissist is a veritable catch-22.

A jail term is useless as a deterrent if it only serves to focus attention on the narcissist. Being infamous is second best to being famous – and far preferable to being ignored. The only way to effectively punish a narcissist is to withhold Narcissistic Supply from him and thus to prevent him from becoming a notorious celebrity.

Given a sufficient amount of media exposure, book contracts, talk shows, lectures, and public attention – the narcissist may even consider the whole grisly affair to be emotionally rewarding. To the narcissist, freedom, wealth, social status, family, vocation – are all means to an end. And the end is attention. If he can secure attention by being the big bad wolf – the narcissist unhesitatingly transforms himself into one. Lord Archer, for instance, seems to be positively basking in the media circus provoked by his prison diaries.

The narcissist does not victimise, plunder, terrorise and abuse others in a cold, calculating manner. He does so offhandedly, as a manifestation of his genuine character. To be truly "guilty" one needs to intend, to deliberate, to contemplate one's choices and then to choose one's acts. The narcissist does none of these.

Thus, punishment breeds in him surprise, hurt and seething anger. The narcissist is stunned by society's insistence that he should be held accountable for his deeds and penalised accordingly. He feels wronged, baffled, injured, the victim of bias, discrimination and injustice. He rebels and rages.

Depending upon the pervasiveness of his magical thinking, the narcissist may feel besieged by overwhelming powers, forces cosmic and intrinsically ominous. He may develop compulsive rites to fend off this "bad", unwarranted, persecutory influences.

The narcissist, very much the infantile outcome of stunted personal development, engages in magical thinking. He feels omnipotent, that there is nothing he couldn't do or achieve if only he sets his mind to it. He feels omniscient – he rarely admits to ignorance and regards his intuitions and intellect as founts of objective data.

Thus, narcissists are haughtily convinced that introspection is a more important and more efficient (not to mention easier to accomplish) method of obtaining knowledge than the systematic study of outside sources of information in accordance with strict and tedious curricula. Narcissists are "inspired" and they despise hamstrung technocrats.

To some extent, they feel omnipresent because they are either famous or about to become famous or because their product is selling or is being manufactured globally. Deeply immersed in their delusions of grandeur, they firmly believe that their acts have – or will have – a great influence not only on their firm, but on their country, or even on Mankind. Having mastered the manipulation of their human environment – they are convinced that they will always "get away with it". They develop hubris and a false sense of immunity.

Narcissistic immunity is the (erroneous) feeling, harboured by the narcissist, that he is impervious to the consequences of his actions, that he will never be effected by the results of his own decisions, opinions, beliefs, deeds and misdeeds, acts, inaction, or membership of certain groups, that he is above reproach and punishment, that, magically, he is protected and will miraculously be saved at the last moment. Hence the audacity, simplicity, and transparency of some of the fraud and corporate looting in the 1990's. Narcissists rarely bother to cover their traces, so great is their disdain and conviction that they are above mortal laws and wherewithal.

What are the sources of this unrealistic appraisal of situations and events?

The False Self is a childish response to abuse and trauma. Abuse is not limited to sexual molestation or beatings. Smothering, doting, pampering, over-indulgence, treating the child as an extension of the parent, not respecting the child's boundaries, and burdening the child with excessive expectations are also forms of abuse.

The child reacts by constructing False Self that is possessed of everything it needs in order to prevail: unlimited and instantaneously available Harry Potter-like powers and wisdom. The False Self, this Superman, is indifferent to abuse and punishment. This way, the child's True Self is shielded from the toddler's harsh reality.

This artificial, maladaptive separation between a vulnerable (but not punishable) True Self and a punishable (but invulnerable) False Self is an effective mechanism. It isolates the child from the unjust, capricious, emotionally dangerous world that he occupies. But, at the same time, it fosters in him a false sense of "nothing can happen to me, because I am not here, I am not available to be punished, hence I am immune to punishment".

The comfort of false immunity is also yielded by the narcissist's sense of entitlement. In his grandiose delusions, the narcissist is sui generis, a gift to humanity, a precious, fragile, object. Moreover, the narcissist is convinced both that this uniqueness is immediately discernible – and that it gives him special rights. The narcissist feels that he is protected by some cosmological law pertaining to "endangered species".

He is convinced that his future contribution to others – his firm, his country, humanity – should and does exempt him from the mundane: daily chores, boring jobs, recurrent tasks, personal exertion, orderly investment of resources and efforts, laws and regulations, social conventions, and so on.

The narcissist is entitled to a "special treatment": high living standards, constant and immediate catering to his needs, the eradication of any friction with the humdrum and the routine, an all-engulfing absolution of his sins, fast track privileges (to higher education, or in his encounters with bureaucracies, for instance). Punishment, trusts the narcissist, is for ordinary people, where no great loss to humanity is involved.

Narcissists are possessed of inordinate abilities to charm, to convince, to seduce, and to persuade. Many of them are gifted orators and intellectually endowed. Many of them work in politics, the media, fashion, show business, the arts, medicine, or business, and serve as religious leaders.

By virtue of their standing in the community, their charisma, or their ability to find the willing scapegoats, they do get exempted many times. Having recurrently "got away with it" – they develop a theory of personal immunity, founded upon some kind of societal and even cosmic "order" in which certain people are above punishment.

But there is a fourth, simpler, explanation. The narcissist lacks self-awareness. Divorced from his True Self, unable to empathise (to understand what it is like to be someone else), unwilling to constrain his actions to cater to the feelings and needs of others – the narcissist is in a constant dreamlike state.

To the narcissist, his life is unreal, like watching an autonomously unfolding movie. The narcissist is a mere spectator, mildly interested, greatly entertained at times. He does not "own" his actions. He, therefore, cannot understand why he should be punished and when he is, he feels grossly wronged.

So convinced is the narcissist that he is destined to great things - that he refuses to accept setbacks, failures and punishments. He regards them as temporary, as the outcomes of someone else's errors, as part of the future mythology of his rise to power/brilliance/wealth/ideal love, etc. Being punished is a diversion of his precious energy and resources from the all-important task of fulfilling his mission in life.

The narcissist is pathologically envious of people and believes that they are equally envious of him. He is paranoid, on guard, ready to fend off an imminent attack. A punishment to the narcissist is a major surprise and a nuisance but it also validates his suspicion that he is being persecuted. It proves to him that strong forces are arrayed against him.

He tells himself that people, envious of his achievements and humiliated by them, are out to get him. He constitutes a threat to the accepted order. When required to pay for his misdeeds, the narcissist is always disdainful and bitter and feels misunderstood by his inferiors.

Cooked books, corporate fraud, bending the (GAAP or other) rules, sweeping problems under the carpet, over-promising, making grandiose claims (the "vision thing") - are hallmarks of a narcissist in action. When social cues and norms encourage such behaviour rather than inhibit it - in other words, when such behaviour elicits abundant Narcissistic Supply - the pattern is reinforced and become entrenched and rigid. Even when circumstances change, the narcissist finds it difficult to adapt, shed his routines, and replace them with new ones. He is trapped in his past success. He becomes a swindler.

But pathological narcissism is not an isolated phenomenon. It is embedded in our contemporary culture. The West's is a narcissistic civilization. It upholds narcissistic values and penalises alternative value-systems. From an early age, children are taught to avoid self-criticism, to deceive themselves regarding their capacities and attainments, to feel entitled, and to exploit others.

As Lilian Katz observed in her important paper, "Distinctions between Self-Esteem and Narcissism: Implications for Practice", published by the Educational Resources Information Centre, the line between enhancing self-esteem and fostering narcissism is often blurred by educators and parents.

Both Christopher Lasch in "The Culture of Narcissism" and Theodore Millon in his books about personality disorders, singled out American society as narcissistic. Litigiousness may be the flip side of an inane sense of entitlement. Consumerism is built on this common and communal lie of "I can do anything I want and possess everything I desire if I only apply myself to it" and on the pathological envy it fosters.

Not surprisingly, narcissistic disorders are more common among men than among women. This may be because narcissism conforms to masculine social mores and to the prevailing ethos of capitalism. Ambition, achievements, hierarchy, ruthlessness, drive - are both social values and narcissistic male traits. Social thinkers like the aforementioned Lasch speculated that modern American culture - a self-centred one - increases the rate of incidence of the Narcissistic Personality Disorder.

Otto Kernberg, a notable scholar of personality disorders, confirmed Lasch's intuition: *"Society can make serious psychological abnormalities, which already exist in some percentage of the population, seem to be at least superficially appropriate."*

In their book "Personality Disorders in Modern Life", Theodore Millon and Roger Davis state, as a matter of fact, that pathological narcissism was once the preserve of "the royal and the wealthy" and that it "seems to have gained prominence only in the late twentieth century". Narcissism, according to them, may be associated with *"higher levels of Maslow's hierarchy of needs ... Individuals in less advantaged nations ... are too busy trying (to survive) ... to be arrogant and grandiose"*.

They - like Lasch before them - attribute pathological narcissism to *"a society that stresses individualism and self-gratification at the expense of community, namely the United States"*. They assert that the disorder is more prevalent among certain professions with "star power" or respect. *"In an individualistic culture, the narcissist is 'God's gift to the world'. In a collectivist society, the narcissist is 'God's gift to the collective'."*

Millon quotes Warren and Caponi's "The Role of Culture in the Development of Narcissistic Personality Disorders in America, Japan and Denmark":

"Individualistic narcissistic structures of self-regard (in individualistic societies) ... are rather self-contained and independent ... (In collectivist cultures) narcissistic configurations

of the we-self ... denote self-esteem derived from strong identification with the reputation and honour of the family, groups, and others in hierarchical relationships."

Still, there are malignant narcissists among subsistence farmers in Africa, nomads in the Sinai desert, day labourers in East Europe, and intellectuals and socialites in Manhattan. Malignant narcissism is all-pervasive and independent of culture and society. It is true, though, that the way pathological narcissism manifests and is experienced is dependent on the particulars of societies and cultures.

In some cultures, it is encouraged, in others suppressed. In some societies it is channelled against minorities – in others it is tainted with paranoia. In collectivist societies, it may be projected onto the collective, in individualistic societies, it is an individual's trait.

Yet, can families, organisations, ethnic groups, churches, and even whole nations be safely described as "narcissistic" or "pathologically self-absorbed"? Can we talk about a "corporate culture of narcissism"?

Human collectives – states, firms, households, institutions, political parties, cliques, bands – acquire a life and a character all their own. The longer the association or affiliation of the members, the more cohesive and conformist the inner dynamics of the group, the more persecutory or numerous its enemies, competitors, or adversaries, the more intensive the physical and emotional experiences of the individuals it is comprised of, the stronger the bonds of locale, language, and history – the more rigorous might an assertion of a common pathology be.

Such an all-pervasive and extensive pathology manifests itself in the behaviour of each and every member. It is a defining – though often implicit or underlying – mental structure. It has explanatory and predictive powers. It is recurrent and invariable – a pattern of conduct melding distorted cognition and stunted emotions. And it is often vehemently denied.

Return

The Professions of the Narcissist

The narcissist naturally gravitates towards those professions which guarantee the abundant and uninterrupted provision of Narcissistic Supply. He seeks to interact with people from a position of authority, advantage, or superiority. He thus elicits their automatic admiration, adulation, and affirmation – or, failing that, their fear and obedience.

Several vocations meet these requirements: teaching, the priesthood, show business, corporate management, the medical professions, politics, and sports. It is safe to predict that narcissists would be over-represented in these occupations.

The cerebral narcissist is likely to emphasise his intellectual prowess and accomplishments (real and imaginary) in an attempt to solicit supply from awe-struck students, devoted parishioners, admiring voters, obsequious subordinates, or dependent patients. His somatic counterpart derives his sense of self-worth from body building, athletic achievements, tests of resilience or endurance, and sexual conquests.

The narcissistic medical doctor or mental health professional and his patients, the narcissistic guide, teacher, or mentor and his students, the narcissistic leader, guru, pundit, or psychic and his followers or admirers, and the narcissistic business tycoon, boss, or employer and his underlings – all are instances of Pathological Narcissistic Spaces.

This is a worrisome state of affairs. Narcissists are liars. They misrepresent their credentials, knowledge, talents, skills, and achievements. A narcissist medical doctor would rather let patients die than expose his ignorance. A narcissistic therapist often traumatises his clients with his acting out, rage, exploitativeness, and lack of empathy. Narcissistic businessmen bring ruin on their firms and employees.

Moreover, even when all is "well", the narcissist's relationship with his sycophants is abusive. He perceives others as objects, mere instruments of gratification, dispensable and interchangeable. An addict, the narcissist tends to pursue an ever-larger dose of adoration, and an ever-bigger fix of attention, while gradually losing what's left of his moral constraints.

When his sources become weary, rebellious, tired, bored, disgusted, repelled, or plainly amused by the narcissist's incessant dependence, his childish craving for attention, his exaggerated or even paranoid fears which lead to obsessive-compulsive behaviours, and his "drama queen" temper tantrums – he resorts to emotional extortion, straight blackmail, abuse, or misuse of his authority, and criminal or antisocial conduct. If these fail, the narcissist devalues and discards the very people he so idealised and cherished only a short while before.

As opposed to their "normal" colleagues or peers, narcissists in authority lack empathy and ethical standards. Thus, they are prone to immorally, cynically, callously and consistently abuse their position. Their socialisation process – usually the product of problematic early relationships with Primary Objects (parents, or caregivers) – is often perturbed and results in social dysfunctioning.

Nor is the narcissist deterred by possible punishment or regards himself subject to Man-made laws. His sense of entitlement coupled with the conviction of his own superiority lead him to believe in his invincibility, invulnerability, immunity, and divinity. The narcissist holds human edicts, rules, and regulations in disdain and human penalties in disdain. He regards human needs and emotions as weaknesses to be predatorily exploited.

Return

The Narcissist
And the Psychopath
In the Workplace

Narcissists in Positions of Authority

Narcissistic Leaders

"It was precisely that evening in Lodi that I came to believe in myself as an unusual person and became consumed with the ambition to do the great things that until then had been but a fantasy."
Napoleon Bonaparte, "Thoughts"

"They may all e called Heroes, in as much as they have derived their purposes and their vocation not from the calm regular course of things, sanctioned by the existing order, but from a concealed fount, from that inner Spirit, still hidden beneath the surface, which impinges on the outer world as a shell and bursts it into pieces - such were Alexander, Caesar, Napoleon ... World-historical men - the Heroes of an epoch - must therefore be recognised as its clear-sighted ones: their deeds, their words are the best of their time ... Moral claims which are irrelevant must not be brought into collision with World-historical deeds ... So mighty a form must trample down many an innocent flower - crush to pieces many an object in its path."
G.W.F. Hegel, "Lectures on the Philosophy of History"

"Such beings are incalculable, they come like fate without cause or reason, inconsiderately and without pretext. Suddenly they are here like lightning too terrible, too sudden, too compelling and too 'different' even to be hated ... What moves them is the terrible egotism of the artist of the brazen glance, who knows himself to be justified for all eternity in his 'work' as the mother is justified in her child ... In all great deceivers a remarkable process is at work to which they owe their power. In the very act of deception with all its preparations, the dreadful voice, expression, and gestures, they are overcome by their belief in

themselves; it is this belief which then speaks, so persuasively, so miracle-like, to the audience."
Friedrich Nietzsche, "The Genealogy of Morals"

"He knows not how to rule a kingdom, that cannot manage a province; nor can he wield a province, that cannot order a city; nor he order a city, that knows not how to regulate a village; nor he a village, that cannot guide a family; nor can that man govern well a family that knows not how to govern himself; neither can any govern himself unless his reason be lord, will and appetite her vassals; nor can reason rule unless herself be ruled by God, and be obedient to Him."
Hugo Grotius

The narcissistic leader is the culmination and reification of his period, culture, and civilisation. He is likely to rise to prominence in narcissistic societies.

The malignant narcissist invents and then projects a False, fictitious, Self for the world to fear, or to admire. He maintains a tenuous grasp on reality to start with and this is further exacerbated by the trappings of power. The narcissist's grandiose self-delusions and fantasies of omnipotence and omniscience are supported by real life authority and the narcissist's predilection to surround himself with obsequious sycophants.

The narcissist's personality is so precariously balanced that he cannot tolerate even a hint of criticism and disagreement. Most narcissists are paranoid and suffer from ideas of reference (the delusion that they are being mocked or discussed when they are not). Thus, narcissists often regard themselves as "victims of persecution".

The narcissistic leader fosters and encourages a personality cult with all the hallmarks of an institutional religion: priesthood, rites, rituals, temples, worship, catechism, mythology. The leader is this religion's ascetic saint. He monastically denies himself earthly pleasures (or so he claims) in order to be able to dedicate himself fully to his calling.

The narcissistic leader is a monstrously inverted Jesus, sacrificing his life and denying himself so that his people – or humanity at large – should benefit. By surpassing and suppressing his humanity, the narcissistic leader became a distorted version of Nietzsche's "superman".

But being a-human or super-human also means being a-sexual and a-moral.

In this restricted sense, narcissistic leaders are post-modernist and moral relativists. They project to the masses an androgynous figure and enhance it by engendering the adoration of nudity and all things "natural" – or by strongly repressing these feelings. But what they refer to as "nature" is not natural at all.

The narcissistic leader invariably proffers an aesthetic of decadence and evil carefully orchestrated and artificial – though it is not perceived this way by him or by his followers. Narcissistic leadership is about reproduced copies, not about originals. It is about the manipulation of symbols – not about veritable atavism or true conservatism.

In short: narcissistic leadership is about theatre, not about life. To enjoy the spectacle (and be subsumed by it), the leader demands the suspension of judgement, depersonalisation, and de-realisation. Catharsis is tantamount, in this narcissistic dramaturgy, to self-annulment.

Narcissism is nihilistic not only operationally, or ideologically. Its very language and narratives are nihilistic. Narcissism is conspicuous nihilism – and the cult's leader serves as a role model, annihilating the Man, only to re-appear as a pre-ordained and irresistible force of nature.

Narcissistic leadership often poses as a rebellion against the "old ways" – against the hegemonic culture, the upper classes, the established religions, the superpowers, the corrupt order. Narcissistic movements are puerile, a reaction to narcissistic injuries inflicted upon a narcissistic (and rather psychopathic) toddler nation-state, or group, or upon the leader.

Minorities or "others" – often arbitrarily selected – constitute a perfect, easily identifiable, embodiment of all that is "wrong". They are accused of being old, they are eerily disembodied, they are cosmopolitan, they are part of the establishment, they are "decadent", they are hated on religious and socio-economic grounds, or because of their race, sexual orientation, origin… They are different, they are narcissistic (feel and act as morally superior), they are everywhere, they are defenceless, they are credulous, they are adaptable (and thus can be co-opted to collaborate in their own destruction). They are the perfect hate figure. Narcissists thrive on hatred and pathological envy.

This is precisely the source of the fascination with Hitler, diagnosed by Erich Fromm – together with Stalin – as a malignant narcissist. He was an inverted human. His unconscious was his conscious. He acted out our most repressed drives, fantasies, and wishes. He provides us with a glimpse of the horrors that lie beneath the veneer, the barbarians at our personal gates, and what it was like before we invented civilisation. Hitler forced us all through a time warp and many did not emerge. He was not the devil. He was one of us. He was what Arendt aptly called the banality of evil. Just an ordinary, mentally disturbed, failure, a member of a mentally disturbed and failing nation, who lived through disturbed and failing times. He was the perfect mirror, a channel, a voice, and the very depth of our souls.

The narcissistic leader prefers the sparkle and glamour of well-orchestrated illusions to the tedium and method of real accomplishments. His reign is all smoke and mirrors, devoid of substances, consisting of mere appearances and mass delusions. In the aftermath of his regime – the narcissistic leader having died, been deposed, or voted out of office – it all unravels. The tireless and constant prestidigitation ceases and the entire edifice crumbles. What looked like an economic miracle turns out to have been a fraud-laced bubble. Loosely-held empires disintegrate. Laboriously assembled business conglomerates go to pieces. "Earth shattering" and "revolutionary" scientific discoveries and theories are discredited. Social experiments end in mayhem.

It is important to understand that the use of violence must be ego-syntonic. It must accord with the self-image of the narcissist. It must abet and sustain his grandiose fantasies and feed his sense of entitlement. It must conform with the narcissistic narrative.

Thus, a narcissist who regards himself as the benefactor of the poor, a member of the common folk, the representative of the disenfranchised, the champion of the dispossessed against the corrupt elite – is highly unlikely to use violence at first.

The pacific mask crumbles when the narcissist has become convinced that the very people he purported to speak for, his constituency, his grassroots fans, the Prime Sources of his Narcissistic Supply – have turned against him. At first, in a desperate effort to maintain the fiction underlying his chaotic personality, the narcissist strives to explain away the sudden reversal of sentiment. "The people are being duped by (the media, big industry, the military, the elite, etc.)", "They don't really know what they are doing", "Following a rude awakening, they will revert to form", etc. When these flimsy attempts to patch a tattered personal mythology fail – the narcissist is injured. Narcissistic injury inevitably leads to narcissistic rage and to a terrifying display of unbridled aggression. The pent-up frustration and hurt translate into devaluation. That which was previously idealised – is now discarded with contempt and hatred.

This primitive defence mechanism is called "splitting". To the narcissist, things and people are either entirely bad (evil) or entirely good. He projects onto others his own shortcomings and negative emotions, thus becoming a totally good object. A narcissistic leader is likely to justify the butchering of his own people by claiming that they intended to kill him, undo the revolution, devastate the economy, or the country, etc.

The "small people", the "rank and file", the "loyal soldiers" of the narcissist - his flock, his nation, his employees - they pay the price. The disillusionment and disenchantment are agonising. The process of reconstruction, of rising from the ashes, of overcoming the trauma of having been deceived, exploited and manipulated - is drawn-out. It is difficult to trust again, to have faith, to love, to be led, to collaborate. Feelings of shame and guilt engulf the erstwhile followers of the narcissist. This is his sole legacy: a massive Post-Traumatic Stress Disorder.

Return

Narcissists in Positions of Authority

Being in a position of authority secures the uninterrupted flow of Narcissistic Supply. Fed by the awe, fear, subordination, admiration, adoration and obedience of his underlings, parish, students, or patients – the narcissist thrives in such circumstances. The narcissist aspires to acquire authority by any means available to him. He may achieve this by making use of some outstanding traits or skills such as his intelligence, or through an asymmetry built into a relationship. The narcissistic medical doctor or mental health professional and his patients, the narcissistic guide, teacher, or mentor and his students, the narcissistic leader, guru, pundit, or psychic and his followers or admirers, or the narcissistic business tycoon, boss, or employer and his subordinates – all are instances of such asymmetries. The rich, powerful, more knowledgeable narcissist occupy a Pathological Narcissistic Space.

These types of relationships – based on the unidirectional and unilateral flow of Narcissistic Supply – border on abuse. The narcissist, in pursuit of an ever-increasing supply, of an ever-larger dose of adoration, and an ever-bigger fix of attention – gradually loses his moral constraints. With time, it gets harder to obtain Narcissistic Supply. The sources of such supply are human and they become weary, rebellious, tired, bored, disgusted, repelled, or plainly amused by the narcissist's incessant dependence, his childish craving for attention, his exaggerated or even paranoid fears which lead to obsessive-compulsive behaviours. To secure their continued collaboration in the procurement of his much-needed supply – the narcissist might resort to emotional extortion, straight blackmail, abuse, or misuse of his authority.

The temptation to do so, though, is universal. No doctor is immune to the charms of certain female patients, nor are university professors asexual. What prevent them from immorally, cynically, callously and consistently abusing their position are ethical imperatives embedded in them through socialisation and empathy. They learned the difference between right and wrong and, having internalised it, they choose right when they face a moral dilemma. They empathise with other human beings, "putting themselves in their shoes", and refrain from doing unto others what they do not wish to be done to them.

It is in these two crucial points that narcissists differ from other humans.

Their socialisation process – usually the product of problematic early relationships with Primary Objects (parents, or caregivers) – is often perturbed and results in social dysfunctioning. And they are incapable of empathising: humans are there only to supply them with Narcissistic Supply. Those unfortunate humans who do not comply with this overriding dictum must be made to alter their ways and if even this fails, the narcissist loses interest in them and they are classified as "sub-human, animals, service-providers, functions, symbols" and worse. Hence the abrupt shifts from over-valuation to devaluation of others. While bearing the gifts of Narcissistic Supply – the "other" is idealised by the narcissist. The narcissist shifts to the opposite pole (devaluation) when Narcissistic Supply dries up or when he estimates that it is about to.

As far as the narcissist is concerned, there is no moral dimension to abusing others – only a pragmatic one: will he be punished for doing so? The narcissist is atavistically responsive to fear and lacks any in-depth understanding of what it is to be a human being. Trapped in his pathology, the narcissist resembles an alien on drugs, a junkie of Narcissistic Supply devoid of the kind of language, which renders human emotions intelligible.

Return

The Narcissist And the Psychopath In the Workplace

Workplace Bullying

Bully at Work

Interview with Tim Field

In 1994 Tim Field was bullied out of his job as a Customer Services Manager which resulted in a stress breakdown. Turning his experience to good use he set up the UK National Workplace Bullying Advice Line in 1996 and his Website Bully Online in 1997 since which time he has worked on over 5000 cases worldwide. He now lectures widely as well as writing and publishing books on bullying and psychiatric injury. He holds two honorary doctorates for his work on identifying and dealing with bullying. He is the Webmaster of Bully Online.

Question: What is workplace bullying?

Answer: Workplace bullying is persistent, unwelcome, intrusive behaviour of one or more individuals whose actions prevent others from fulfilling their duties.

Question: How is it different to adopting disciplinarian measures, maintaining strict supervision, or oversight?

Answer: The purpose of bullying is to hide the inadequacy of the bully and has nothing to do with "management" or the achievement of tasks. Bullies project their inadequacies onto others to distract and divert attention away from the inadequacies. In most cases of workplace bullying reported to the UK National Workplace Bullying Advice Line, the bully is a serial bully who has a history of conflict with staff. The bullying that one sees is often also the tip of an iceberg of wrongdoing which may include misappropriation of budgets, harassment, discrimination, as well as breaches of rules, regulations, professional codes of conduct and health and safety practices.

Question: Should it be distinguished from harassment (including sexual harassment), or stalking?

Answer: Bullying is, I believe, the underlying behaviour and thus the common denominator of harassment, discrimination, stalking and abuse. What varies is the focus for expression of the behaviour. For instance, a harasser or discriminator focuses on race or gender or disability.

Bullies focus on competence and popularity which at present are not covered by employment legislation.

Bullies seethe with resentment and anger and the conduits for release of this inner anger are jealousy and envy which explains why bullies pick on employees who are good at their job and popular with people. Being emotionally immature, bullies crave attention and become resentful when others get more attention for their competence and achievements than themselves.

Question: What is the profile of the typical bully?

Answer: Over 90% of the cases reported to the UK National Workplace Bullying Advice Line involve a serial bully who can be recognised by their behaviour profile which includes compulsive lying, a Jekyll and Hyde nature, an unusually high verbal facility, charm and a considerable capacity to deceive, an arrested level of emotional development, and a compulsive need to control. The serial bully rarely commits a physical assault or an arrestable offence, preferring instead to remain within the realms of psychological violence and non-arrestable offences.

Question: What are bullying's typical outcomes?

Answer: In the majority of cases, the target of bullying is eliminated through forced resignation, unfair dismissal, or early or ill – health retirement whilst the bully is promoted. After a short interval of between 2-14 days, the bully selects another target and the cycle restarts. Sometimes another target is selected before the current target is eliminated.

Question: Can you provide us with some statistics? How often does bullying occur? How many people are affected?

Answer: Surveys of bullying in the UK indicate that between 12-50% of the workforce experience bullying. Statistics from the UK National Workplace Bullying Advice Line reveal that around 20% of cases are from the education sector, 12% are from healthcare, 10% are from social services, and around 6% from the voluntary / charity / not-for-profit sector.

After that, calls come from all sectors both public and private, with finance, media, police, postal workers and other government employees featuring prominently. Enquiries from outside the UK (notably USA, Canada, Australia and Ireland) show similar patterns with the caring professions topping the list of bullied workers.

Question: Could you estimate the economic effects of workplace bullying – costs to employers (firms), employees, law enforcement agencies, the courts, the government, etc.?

Answer: Bullying is one of the major causes of stress, and the cost of stress to UK plc is thought to be between £5-12 billion (US$7-17 billion). When all the direct, indirect and consequential costs of bullying are taken into account, the cost to UK plc (taxpayers and shareholders) could be in excess of £30 billion (US$44 billion), equivalent to around £1,000 hidden tax per working adult per year. Employers do not account for the cost of bullying and its consequences, therefore the figures never appear on balance sheets.

Employees have to work twice as hard to overcome the serial bully's inefficiency and dysfunction which can spread through an organisation like a cancer.

Because of its subtle nature, bullying can be difficult to recognise, but the consequences are easy to spot: excessive workloads, lack of support, a climate of fear, and high levels of insecurity.

The effects on health include, amongst other things, chronic fatigue, damage to the immune system, reactive depression, and suicide.

The indirect costs of bullying include higher-than average staff turnover and sickness absence. Each of these incur consequential costs of staff cover, administration, loss of production and reduced productivity which are rarely recognised and even more rarely attributed to their cause. Absenteeism alone costs UK plc over £10 billion a year and stress is now officially the number one cause of sickness absence having taken over from the common cold. However, surveys suggest that at least 20% of employers still do not regard stress as a health and safety issue, instead preferring to see it as skiving and malingering.

The Bristol Stress and Health at Work Study published by the HSE in June 2000 revealed that 1 in 5 UK workers (around 5.5m) reported feeling extremely stressed at work. The main stress factors were having too much work and not being supported by managers. In November 2001 a study by Proudfoot Consulting revealed the cost of bad management, low employee morale and poorly-trained staff to British business at 117 lost working days a year. At 65%, bad management (often a euphemism for bullying) accounted for the biggest slice of unproductive days with low morale accounting for 17%. The study also suggested that in the

UK 52% of all working time is spent unproductively compared to the European average of 43%.

The results of a three-year survey of British workers by the Gallup Organisation published in October 2001 revealed that many employers are not getting the best from their employees. The most common response to questions such as "How engaged are your employees?" and "How effective is your leadership and management style?" and "How well are you capitalising on the talents, skills and knowledge of your people?" was an overwhelming "Not very much". The survey also found that the longer an employee stayed, the less engaged they became. The cost to UK plc of lost work days due to lack of engagement was estimated to be between £39-48 billion a year.

Question: What can be done to reduce workplace bullying? Are firms, the government, law enforcement agencies, the courts - aware of the problem and its magnitude? Are educational campaign effective? Did anti-bullying laws prove effective?

Answer: Most bullying is hierarchical and can be traced to the top or near the top. As bullying is often the visible tip of an iceberg of wrongdoing, denial is the most common strategy employed by toxic managements. Only Sweden has a law which specifically addresses bullying. Where no law exists, bullies feel free to bully. Whilst the law is not a solution, the presence of a law is an indication that society has made a judgement that the behaviour is no longer acceptable.

Awareness of bullying, and especially its seriousness, is still low throughout society. Bullying is not just "something children do in the playground", it's a lifetime behaviour on the same level as domestic violence, sexual harassment, and rape.

Bullying is a form of psychological and emotional rape because of its intrusive and violational nature.

Return

Narcissism in the Workplace

Online Conference Transcript
HelthyPlace.com

David: Good Evening. I hope your day went well. Welcome to HealthyPlace.com and our chat conference on "Narcissism in the Workplace". I'm David Roberts, the moderator of tonight's chat. Some of the topics we'll be discussing include: How to cope with a narcissistic boss, co-worker, supplier, colleague, partner, competitor, manager, or employee. And when is it time to toss in the towel and leave that troublesome job?

Our guest, Dr. Sam Vaknin, has a Ph.D. in philosophy and is the author of the book Malignant Self Love - Narcissism Revisited. We discussed various aspects of narcissism in the workplace, including how to recognise a narcissist, what personality types can work with a narcissist and how to cope with a narcissistic employer.

Just to clarify, Dr. Vaknin is not a therapist or medical doctor of any sort. However, he is an expert on the subject of narcissism and a self-proclaimed narcissist.

Good Evening Dr. Vaknin and welcome to HealthyPlace.com. Just so we are all clear on the subject, can you give us a brief overview of what narcissism is?

Dr. Vaknin: Great to be here again. Thank you for having me and for the kind words. Hello, everyone.

Narcissists are driven by the need to uphold and maintain a False Self. They use the False Self to garner Narcissistic Supply which is any kind of attention adulation, admiration, or even notoriety and infamy.

David: How does one recognise a narcissist?

Dr. Vaknin: It is close to impossible and that is the secret of their astounding success. Narcissists are good actors. They are adept at charming others, persuading them, manipulating them, or otherwise influencing them to do their bidding. The narcissist's sense of self-worth is unstable (labile) so, the narcissist relies on input from other people to regulate his self-esteem and self-confidence. He focuses on potential Sources of Supply and engulfs them with focused attention and simulated deep emotions. Only in later encounter, as time passes and the number of interactions grows, is it possible to tell that someone is a narcissist. Narcissists are preoccupied with grandiose fantasies unrealistic plans. They are poor judges of reality. They are bullies and often resort to verbal and emotional abuse. They exploit people and then discard them. They have no empathy and regard their co-workers as mere instruments objects, tools, and sources of adulation, affirmation, or potential benefits.

David: So, in the beginning, you are saying they will get on your good side by charming you and pretending to be interested in you and what you're doing. Later, what kind of behaviours should a person expect from the: (1) narcissistic boss and (2) colleague? And I'm assuming here that the behaviours for the two might be different.

Dr. Vaknin: Workplace narcissists seethe with anger and resentment. The gap between reality and their grandiose flights of fancy (the Grandiosity Gap) is so great that they develop persecutory delusions, resentment and rage. They are also extremely and pathologically envious, seeking to destroy what they perceive to be the sources of their constant frustration: a popular co-worker, a successful boss, a qualified or skilled employee. Narcissists at work crave constant attention and will go to great lengths to secure it - including by "engineering" situations that place them at the centre. They are immature, constantly nagging and complaining, finding fault with everyone and everything, Cassandras who constantly predict impending doom. They are intrusive and invasive. They firmly believe in their own omnipotence and omniscience. They feel entitled to special treatment and are convinced that they are above Man-made laws, including the rules of their place of employment. They are very disruptive, poor team members, can rarely collaborate with others without being cantankerous and quarrelsome. They are control freaks and feel the compulsive and irresistible urge to interfere in everything to micromanage and overrule others. All in all, a highly unpleasant experience.

David: If you work with or under a narcissist, it sounds like your work life might be a living hell.

Dr. Vaknin: You would never forget it. It is traumatic and very likely to end in actual bullying and stalking behaviours. Many workers end up with PTSD – Post Traumatic Stress Syndrome. Others quit, or even relocate.

David: What kind of individual, personality-wise, is best suited to work with a narcissist co-worker or boss?

Dr. Vaknin: Certain pathological personalities – for instance, someone with a Dependent Personality Disorder – or an Inverted Narcissist may get along just fine. A submissive person whose expectations are limited, moods are subdued and willingness to absorb abuse is extended would survive with a narcissist, or even thrive in such an environment. But the vast majority of workers are likely to suffer ill-health effects, clash with the narcissist, or end up being sacked, reassigned, relocated, or demoted. The narcissistic bully very often gets his way: He gets promoted, the ideas he "adopted" become corporate policy, his misdeeds are overlooked, his misbehaviour tolerated. This is partly because, as I said earlier, narcissists are excellent liars with considerable thespian skills – and partly because no one wants to mess around with a thug, even if his thuggery is limited to words and gestures.

David: We have a lot of audience questions, Dr. Vaknin. Let's get to a few and then I have a few more questions to ask you. Here's the first one:

AMichael: How common is narcissism within the population?

Dr. Vaknin: According to orthodoxy, between 0.7%-1% of the adult population suffer from the Narcissistic Personality Disorder. This figure is an underestimate. Pathological narcissism is under-reported because, by definition, few narcissists admit that anything is wrong with them and that they may be the source of the constant problem in their life and the lives of their nearest or dearest. Narcissists resort to therapy only in the wake of a harrowing life crisis. They have alloplastic defences – they tend to blame the world, their boss, society, God, their spouse for their misfortune and failures. Last, but not least, psychotherapists regard narcissists as "difficult" patients with a "severe" personality disorder – or, put plainly, lots of work with little reward. Narcissists, Paranoiacs and Psychotherapists, Narcissistic Personality Disorder (NPD) At a Glance.

Doria57: Is there any way to get along with these type of people at work?

Dr. Vaknin: Here are a few useful guidelines:
1. Never disagree with the narcissist or contradict him.

2. Never offer him any intimacy. You are not his equal and an offer of intimacy insultingly implies that you are.

3. Look awed by whatever attribute matters to him (for instance: by his professional achievements or by his good looks, or by his success with women and so on).

4. Never remind him of life outside his bubble and if you do, connect it somehow to his sense of grandiosity. Do not make any comment, which might directly or indirectly impinge on his self-image, omnipotence, judgement, omniscience, skills, capabilities, professional record, or even omnipresence.

5. Bad sentences start with: "I think you overlooked & made a mistake here & you don't know & do you know & you were not here yesterday so & you cannot & you should", etc. These are perceived as rude imposition. Narcissists react very badly to restrictions placed on their freedom.

Linda3003: My husband is employed by a very large university, in spite of "outstanding" appraisals, many stolen ideas, marked increase in customer satisfaction and being very professional, he was recently fired. His boss did not like the acolaides my husband was receiving, etc. How does one combat the defamation?

Dr. Vaknin: Depends on your resources and your ability to accept recurrent interim defeats. Narcissistic bosses are very tenacious and resourceful. They are pillars of the community, usually widely respected and believed. They have at their disposal the entire wherewithal of the organisation. People say "Where there's fire, there's smoke". "If he was fired, there must have been a good reason for it", "Why couldn't he simply get along? He must be egocentric, a bad team player". And so on. It is un uphill battle. My advice to you is to team up with an anti-bullying group or to have an attorney look into wrongful dismissal charges.

Here is an excellent place to start your search:

http://www.bullyonline.org/workbully/npd.htm,

http://www.bullyonline.org/workbully/

freedom03: I would like to know if the narcissist is aware of what they are doing?

Dr. Vaknin: Aware, cunning, premeditated, and, sometimes, even enjoying every bit of it. But it is not malice that drives them. They believe in their own destiny, superiority, entitlement, exemption from laws promulgated by mere mortals. The narcissist regards himself as one would an expensive present, a gift to his company, to his family, to his neighbours, to his colleagues, to his country. Resistance calls for strenuous measures. Disagreement with the narcissist is bound to be the outcome of ignorance or obstructionism. Criticism is malevolent and ill-founded. The narcissist trusts that he has the full moral justification to battle his foes. To his mind, the world is a hostile place, full of Lilliputians who seek to shackle his genius, foresight, and natural advantages. They aim to harness and castrate – and they deserve his ire and the ensuing punishment he metes out to them in his infinite wisdom. It is a crusade against the injustice of not recognising the narcissist's true place in this world – at the pinnacle.

David: Dr. Vaknin, earlier you mention that the narcissist would act empathetic to draw in his prey, so to speak. In light of that, here's the next question:

martha j: Can this person genuinely develop authentic empathy skills?

Dr. Vaknin: No, he cannot. Narcissists lack the basic machinery of putting themselves in other people's shoes. They react with fury and denial when confronted with the fact that persons in their environments are individual entities with their own idiosyncratic and specific needs, preferences, choices, fears, hopes, and expectations. This, the refusal to grant autonomy, is at the core of abuse, whether on the domestic front or at the workplace. To the narcissist, others are mere extensions, instruments of gratification, sources of narcissistic supply. And nothing more than that.

delaware1974: With so many people afflicted with this – why are we making it sound like a death sentence? All of us still need to move on with our lives ... are we supposed to give up and accept because it's hard? We spend a lot of time talking about the negative or "escaping" the narcissist, "surviving" the narcissist, what about those of us that want to help them and NOT give up on them? Are there LIVE face-to-face help groups? Hope?

Dr. Vaknin: It is possible to live with the narcissist, as I made clear earlier. It requires certain behavioural modifications and a willingness to accept the narcissist largely as he is. These may be of interest:

The Inverted Narcissist
Treatment Modalities and Psychotherapies
The Reconditioned Narcissist
Narcissists, Paranoiacs and Psychotherapists
Narcissist Employer

And, yes, there are groups (though only online) who tackle healing and co-existence – they are listed here.

I am not aware of a live group though I heard recently that something is being organised in New York. Bullying – and especially workplace bullying – is tackled by many online and live groups. This Website, managed by a former bullying victim, Tim Field, is the best I know of. It contains links to hundreds of resources.

David: For many people, Dr. Vaknin, if you are in a situation working with a narcissist or under a narcissist, they can't just pick up and leave their job. What is the best way for them to cope without "kissing" up to this person and being always vigilant about what you say and how you say it? or is that the only way to survive?

Dr. Vaknin: It depends whether the narcissistic bully represents the corporate culture of the workplace – or is an isolated case attributable to a quirky nature or a personality disorder. Alas, very often, abusive behaviours in one's office or shop floor are merely the epitome of all-pervasive wrongdoing which permeates the entire hierarchy, from top management to the bottom rung of employment. Bullies rarely dare to express their tendencies in isolation and in defiance of the prevailing ethos. Or, if they do run against the grain of their place of employment, they lose their jobs. Typically, narcissists join already narcissistic firms and mesh well with a toxic workplace, a poisonous atmosphere, and an abusive management. If one is not willing to succumb to the mores and (lack of) ethics of the workplace, there is little one can do. Surprisingly few countries (Sweden, the United Kingdom, to some extent) outlaw workplace abuse specifically. Whistleblowers and "troublemakers" are frowned upon and are not protected by any institutions. It is a dismal landscape. The victim would do well to simply resign and move on, sad as this may be. As awareness of the phenomenon increases and laws take effect, hopefully this will change and bullied and abused workers will find effective ways to cope with mistreatment.

TimeToFly: What typically happens to a narcissist when they lose their position of authority or their job. How do they react to that? My narcissist ex-husband recently lost his job. He will not say what happened exactly, typical. But since then he has been on a rampage to destroy me. It was right after the loss of his previous job that he left me and our children 4 years ago. He had been the manager of engineering and was first demoted, and then finally left the company. I never did get the story. He has just remarried, but his new life somehow has not distracted him from his obsession with destroying mine.

Dr. Vaknin: Being demoted or losing one's job is a narcissistic injury (or wound). The entire edifice of the Narcissistic Personality Disorder is an elaborate and multi-layered reaction to past narcissistic injuries. A gap opens between the way the narcissistic imagines himself to be (grandiosity) and reality (unemployed, humiliated, discarded, unneeded). The narcissist strives to bridge the Grandiosity Gap but sometimes it is simply to abysmal to deny or ignore. So, some narcissists go through decompensation - their defence mechanisms crumble. They may even experience brief psychotic episodes. They become dysfunctional. The narcissists redouble their efforts to obtain Narcissistic Supply by any means - sex, exercise, attention-seeking behaviours. Yet others withdraw altogether to "lick their wounds" (schizoid posture). What is common to all these narcissists is the ominous feeling that they are losing control (and maybe even losing it). In a desperate effort to re-exert control, the narcissist becomes abusive. Sometimes abuse is about controlling the victim. Others seek "easy targets" - lonely women to "conquer" or simple tasks to accomplish, or no-brainers, or to compete against weak opponents with a guaranteed result.

For more on these behaviours:

What is Abuse?

The Delusional Way Out

Deficient Narcissistic Supply

David: If you are interested in purchasing Dr. Vaknin's excellent and very thorough book on narcissism, Malignant Self Love: Narcissism Revisited, click on the link.

jenmosaic: What causes NPD?

Dr. Vaknin: No one knows. The accepted wisdom is that NPD is tan adaptative reaction to early childhood or early adolescence trauma and abuse. There are many forms of abuse. The more familiar ones - verbal, emotional, psychological, physical, sexual - of course yield psychopathologies. But are far more subtle and more insidious forms of mistreatment. Doting, smothering, ignoring personal boundaries, treating someone as an extension or a wish-fulfilment machine, spoiling, emotional blackmail, an ambience of paranoia or intimidation ("gaslighting") - have as long lasting effects as the "classic" varieties of abuse. Still, there is always the possibility of a hereditary component. More about the roots of narcissism here.

David: Here are a couple of audience comments about what's been said tonight:

Doria57: No one ever wants to form an anti-bullying group, they are afraid.

martha j: The descriptions of the narcissistic boss - Isn't this the unfortunate all American definition of the "successful boss"?

Dr. Vaknin: I'd like to respond to that last comment. Mental health disorders - and especially personality disorders - are not divorced from the twin contexts of culture and society. Western society and culture are narcissistic. Disparate scholars and thinkers - Christopher Lasch on the one hand and Theodore Millon on the other hand - have concluded as much. Narcissistic behaviours - now labelled "misconduct" - have long been nornmative. The basically narcissistic traits of individualism competitiveness, unbridled ambition - are the founding stones of certain versions of capitalism. Thus, certain forms of abuse and bullying actually constitute an integral part of the folklore of corporate America. Narcissistic bosses were idolised. As long as this is the case, workplace abuse would be hard to overcome. More here:

Collective Narcissism
Narcissistic Leaders
Narcissism in the Boardroom
Bully at Work Interview with Tim Field

David: Thank you, Dr. Vaknin, for being our guest this evening and for sharing this information with us. And to those in the audience, thank you for coming and participating. I hope you found it helpful. We have a very large and active community here at HealthyPlace.com. You will always find people in the chat rooms and interacting with various sites. Also, if you found our site beneficial, I hope you'll pass our URL around to your friends, mail list buddies, and others.

Return

The Narcissist
And the Psychopath
In the Workplace

Celebrity Narcissists

The Narcissist's Addiction to Fame and Celebrity

Narcissists are addicted to being famous. This, by far, is their predominant drive. Being famous encompasses a few important functions: it endows the narcissist with power, provides him with a constant Source of Narcissistic Supply (admiration, adoration, approval, awe), and fulfils important ego functions.

The image that the narcissist projects is hurled back at him, reflected by those exposed to his celebrity or fame. This way he feels alive, his very existence is affirmed and he acquires a sensation of clear boundaries (where the narcissist ends and the world begins).

There is a set of narcissistic behaviours typical to the pursuit of celebrity. There is almost nothing that the narcissist refrains from doing, almost no borders that he hesitates to cross to achieve renown. To him, there is no such thing as "bad publicity" – what matters is to be in the public eye.

Because the narcissist equally enjoys all types of attention and likes as much to be feared as to be loved, for instance – he doesn't mind if what is published about him is wrong ("As long as they spell my name correctly"). The narcissist's only bad emotional stretches are during periods of lack of attention, publicity, or exposure.

The narcissist then feels empty, hollowed out, negligible, humiliated, wrathful, discriminated against, deprived, neglected, treated unjustly and so on. At first, he tries to obtain attention from ever narrowing groups of reference ("supply scale down"). But the feeling that he is compromising gnaws at his anyhow fragile self-esteem.

Sooner or later, the spring bursts. The narcissist plots, contrives, plans, conspires, thinks, analyses, synthesises and does whatever else is necessary to regain the lost exposure in the public eye. The more he fails to secure the attention of the target group (always the largest) – the more daring, eccentric and outlandish he becomes. Firm decision to become known is transformed into resolute action and then to a panicky pattern of attention seeking behaviours.

The narcissist is not really interested in publicity per se. Narcissists are misleading. The narcissist appears to love himself – and, really, he abhors himself. Similarly, he appears to be interested in becoming a celebrity – and, in reality, he is concerned with the REACTIONS to his fame: people watch him, notice him, talk about him, debate his actions – therefore he exists.

The narcissist goes around "hunting and collecting" the way the expressions on people's faces change when they notice him. He places himself at the centre of attention, or even as a figure of controversy. He constantly and recurrently pesters those nearest and dearest to him in a bid to reassure himself that he is not losing his fame, his magic touch, the attention of his social milieu.

Truly, the narcissist is not choosy. If he can become famous as a writer – he writes, if as a businessman – he conducts business. He switches from one field to the other with ease and without remorse because in all of them he is present without conviction, bar the conviction that he must (and deserves to) get famous.

He grades activities, hobbies and people not according to the pleasure that they give him – but according to their utility: can they or can't they make him known and, if so, to what extent. The narcissist is one-track minded (not to say obsessive). His is a world of black (being unknown and deprived of attention) and white (being famous and celebrated).

Return

Mistreating Celebrities

An Interview Granted to Superinteressante Magazine in Brazil

Question: Fame and TV shows about celebrities usually have a huge audience. This is understandable: people like to see other successful people. But why people like to see celebrities being humiliated?

Answer: As far as their fans are concerned, celebrities fulfil two emotional functions: they provide a mythical narrative (a story that the fan can follow and identify with) and they function as blank screens onto which the fans project their dreams, hopes, fears, plans, values, and desires (wish fulfilment). The slightest deviation from these prescribed roles provokes enormous rage and makes us want to punish (humiliate) the "deviant" celebrities.

But why?

When the human foibles, vulnerabilities, and frailties of a celebrity are revealed, the fan feels humiliated, "cheated", hopeless, and "empty". To reassert his self-worth, the fan must establish his or her moral superiority over the erring and "sinful" celebrity. The fan must "teach the celebrity a lesson" and show the celebrity "who's boss". It is a primitive defence mechanism – narcissistic grandiosity. It puts the fan on equal footing with the exposed and "naked" celebrity.

Question: This taste for watching a person being humiliated has something to do with the attraction to catastrophes and tragedies?

Answer: There is always a sadistic pleasure and a morbid fascination in vicarious suffering. Being spared the pains and tribulations others go through makes the observer feel "chosen", secure, and virtuous. The higher celebrities rise, the harder they fall. There is something gratifying in hubris defied and punished.

Question: Do you believe the audience put themselves in the place of the reporter (when he asks something embarrassing to a celebrity) and become in some way revenged?

Answer: The reporter "represents" the "bloodthirsty" public. Belittling celebrities or watching their comeuppance is the modern equivalent of the gladiator rink. Gossip used to fulfil the same function and now the mass media broadcast live the slaughtering of fallen gods. There is no question of revenge here - just Schadenfreude, the guilty joy of witnessing your superiors penalised and "cut down to size".

Question: In your country, who are the celebrities people love to hate?

Answer: Israelis like to watch politicians and wealthy businessmen reduced, demeaned, and slighted. In Macedonia, where I live, all famous people, regardless of their vocation, are subject to intense, proactive, and destructive envy. This love-hate relationship with their idols, this ambivalence, is attributed by psychodynamic theories of personal development to the child's emotions towards his parents. Indeed, we transfer and displace many negative emotions we harbour onto celebrities.

Question: I would never dare asking some questions the reporters from Panico ask the celebrities. What are the characteristics of people like these reporters?

Answer: Sadistic, ambitious, narcissistic, lacking empathy, self-righteous, pathologically and destructively envious, with a fluctuating sense of self-worth (possibly an inferiority complex).

Question: Do you believe the actors and reporters want themselves to be as famous as the celebrities they tease? Because I think this is almost happening...

Answer: The line is very thin. Newsmakers and newsmen and women are celebrities merely because they are public figures and regardless of their true accomplishments. A celebrity is famous for being famous. Of course, such journalists will likely to fall prey to up and coming colleagues in an endless and self-perpetuating food chain...

Question: I think that the fan-celebrity relationship gratifies both sides. What are the advantages the fans get and what are the advantages the celebrities get?

Answer: There is an implicit contract between a celebrity and his fans. The celebrity is obliged to "act the part", to fulfil the expectations of his admirers, not to deviate from the roles that they impose and he or she accepts. In return the fans shower the celebrity with adulation. They idolise him or her and make him or her feel omnipotent, immortal, "larger than life", omniscient, superior, and sui generis (unique).

What are the fans getting for their trouble?

Above all, the ability to vicariously share the celebrity's fabulous (and, usually, partly confabulated) existence. The celebrity becomes their "representative" in fantasyland, their extension and proxy, the reification and embodiment of their deepest desires and most secret and guilty dreams. Many celebrities are also role models or father/mother figures. Celebrities are proof that there is more to life than drab and routine. That beautiful - nay, perfect - people do exist and that they do lead charmed lives. There's hope yet - this is the celebrity's message to his fans.

The celebrity's inevitable downfall and corruption is the modern-day equivalent of the medieval morality play. This trajectory - from rags to riches and fame and back to rags or worse - proves that order and justice do prevail, that hubris invariably gets punished, and that the celebrity is no better, neither is he superior, to his fans.

Question: Why are celebrities narcissists? How is this disorder born?

Answer: No one knows if pathological narcissism is the outcome of inherited traits, the sad result of abusive and traumatising upbringing, or the confluence of both. Often, in the same family, with the same set of parents and an identical emotional environment - some siblings grow to be malignant narcissists, while others are perfectly "normal". Surely, this indicates a genetic predisposition of some people to develop narcissism.

It would seem reasonable to assume - though, at this stage, there is not a shred of proof - that the narcissist is born with a propensity to develop narcissistic defences. These are triggered by abuse or trauma during the formative years in infancy or during early adolescence. By "abuse" I am referring to a spectrum of behaviours which objectify the child and treat it as an extension of the caregiver (parent) or as a mere instrument of gratification. Dotting and smothering are as abusive as beating and starving. And abuse can be dished out by peers as well as by parents, or by adult role models.

Not all celebrities are narcissists. Still, some of them surely are.

We all search for positive cues from people around us. These cues reinforce in us certain behaviour patterns. There is nothing special in the fact that the narcissist-celebrity does the same. However there are two major differences between the narcissistic and the normal personality.

The first is quantitative. The normal person is likely to welcome a moderate amount of attention – verbal and non-verbal – in the form of affirmation, approval, or admiration. Too much attention, though, is perceived as onerous and is avoided. Destructive and negative criticism is avoided altogether.

The narcissist, in contrast, is the mental equivalent of an alcoholic. He is insatiable. He directs his whole behaviour, in fact his life, to obtain these pleasurable titbits of attention. He embeds them in a coherent, completely biased, picture of himself. He uses them to regulates his labile (fluctuating) sense of self-worth and self-esteem.

To elicit constant interest, the narcissist projects on to others a confabulated, fictitious version of himself, known as the False Self. The False Self is everything the narcissist is not: omniscient, omnipotent, charming, intelligent, rich, or well-connected.

The narcissist then proceeds to harvest reactions to this projected image from family members, friends, co-workers, neighbours, business partners and from colleagues. If these – the adulation, admiration, attention, fear, respect, applause, affirmation – are not forthcoming, the narcissist demands them, or extorts them. Money, compliments, a favourable critique, an appearance in the media, a sexual conquest are all converted into the same currency in the narcissist's mind, into Narcissistic Supply.

So, the narcissist is not really interested in publicity per se or in being famous. Truly he is concerned with the REACTIONS to his fame: how people watch him, notice him, talk about him, debate his actions. It "proves" to him that he exists.

The narcissist goes around "hunting and collecting" the way the expressions on people's faces change when they notice him. He places himself at the centre of attention, or even as a figure of controversy. He constantly and recurrently pesters those nearest and dearest to him in a bid to reassure himself that he is not losing his fame, his magic touch, the attention of his social milieu.

Return

Acquired Situational Narcissism

The Narcissistic Personality Disorder (NPD) is a systemic, all-pervasive condition, very much like pregnancy: either you have it or you don't. Once you have it, you have it day and night, it is an inseparable part of the personality, a recurrent set of behaviour patterns.

Recent research (1996) by Roningstam and others, however, shows that there is a condition which might be called "Transient or Temporary or Short-Term Narcissism" as opposed to the full-fledged version. Even prior to their discovery, "Reactive Narcissistic Regression" was well known: people regress to a transient narcissistic phase in response to a major life crisis which threatens their mental composure.

Reactive or transient narcissism may also be triggered by medical or organic conditions. Brain injuries, for instance, have been known to induce narcissistic and antisocial traits and behaviours.

But can narcissism be acquired or learned? Can it be provoked by certain, well-defined, situations?

Robert B. Millman, professor of psychiatry at New York Hospital – Cornell Medical School thinks it can. He proposes to reverse the accepted chronology. According to him, pathological narcissism can be induced in adulthood by celebrity, wealth, and fame.

The "victims" – billionaire tycoons, movie stars, renowned authors, politicians, and other authority figures – develop grandiose fantasies, lose their erstwhile ability to empathise, react with rage to slights, both real and imagined and, in general, act like textbook narcissists.

But is the occurrence of Acquired Situational Narcissism (ASN) inevitable and universal - or are only certain people prone to it?

It is likely that ASN is merely an amplification of earlier narcissistic conduct, traits, style, and tendencies. Celebrities with ASN already had a narcissistic personality and have acquired it long before it "erupted". Being famous, powerful, or rich only "legitimised" and conferred immunity from social sanction on the unbridled manifestation of a pre-existing disorder. Indeed, narcissists tend to gravitate to professions and settings which guarantee fame, celebrity, power, and wealth.

As Millman correctly notes, the celebrity's life is abnormal. The adulation is often justified and plentiful, the feedback biased and filtered, the criticism muted and belated, social control either lacking or excessive and vitriolic. Such vicissitudinal existence is not conducive to mental health even in the most balanced person.

The confluence of a person's narcissistic predisposition and his pathological life circumstances gives rise to ASN. Acquired Situational Narcissism borrows elements from both the classic Narcissistic Personality Disorder – ingrained and all-pervasive – and from Transient or Reactive Narcissism.

Celebrities are, therefore, unlikely to "heal" once their fame or wealth or might are gone. Instead, their basic narcissism merely changes form. It continues unabated, as insidious as ever – but modified by life's ups and downs.

In a way, all narcissistic disturbances are acquired. Patients acquire their pathological narcissism from abusive or overbearing parents, from peers, and from role models. Narcissism is a defence mechanism designed to fend off hurt and danger brought on by circumstances – such as celebrity – beyond the person's control.

Social expectations play a role as well. Celebrities try to conform to the stereotype of a creative but spoiled, self-centred, monomaniacal, and emotive individual. A tacit trade takes place. We offer the famous and the powerful all the Narcissistic Supply they crave – and they, in turn, act the consummate, fascinating albeit repulsive, narcissists.

Return

The Narcissist
And the Psychopath
In the Workplace

Narcissists and God
The Religious Narcissist

For the Love of God

"1 But know this, that in the last days perilous times will come: 2 For men will be lovers of themselves, lovers of money, boasters, proud, blasphemers, disobedient to parents, unthankful, unholy, 3 unloving, unforgiving, slanderers, without self-control, brutal, despisers of good, 4 traitors, headstrong, haughty, lovers of pleasure rather than lovers of God, 5 having a form of godliness but denying its power. And from such people turn away! 6 For of this sort are those who creep into households and make captives of gullible women loaded down with sins, led away by various lusts, 7 always learning and never able to come to the knowledge of the truth. 8 Now as Jan'nes and Jam'bres resisted Moses, so do these also resist the truth: men of corrupt minds, disapproved concerning the faith; 9 but they will progress no further, for their folly will be manifest to all, as theirs also was."
The Second Epistle of Paul the Apostle to Timothy 3:1-9

God is everything the narcissist ever wants to be: omnipotent, omniscient, omnipresent, admired, much discussed, and awe inspiring. God is the narcissist's wet dream, his ultimate grandiose fantasy. But God comes handy in other ways as well.

The narcissist alternately idealises and devalues figures of authority.

In the idealisation phase, he strives to emulate them, he admires them, imitate them (often ludicrously), and defends them. They cannot go wrong, or be wrong. The narcissist regards them as bigger than life, infallible, perfect, whole, and brilliant. But as the narcissist's unrealistic and inflated expectations are inevitably frustrated, he begins to devalue his former idols.

Now they are "human" (to the narcissist, a derogatory term). They are small, fragile, error-prone, pusillanimous, mean, dumb, and mediocre. The narcissist goes through the same cycle in his relationship with God, the quintessential authority figure.

But often, even when disillusionment and iconoclastic despair have set in - the narcissist continues to pretend to love God and follow Him. The narcissist maintains this deception because his continued proximity to God confers on him authority. Priests, leaders of the congregation, preachers, evangelists, cultists, politicians, intellectuals - all derive authority from their allegedly privileged relationship with God.

Religious authority allows the narcissist to indulge his sadistic urges and to exercise his misogynism freely and openly. Such a narcissist is likely to taunt and torment his followers, hector and chastise them, humiliate and berate them, abuse them spiritually, or even sexually.

The narcissist whose source of authority is religious is looking for obedient and unquestioning slaves upon whom to exercise his capricious and wicked mastery. The narcissist transforms even the most innocuous and pure religious sentiments into a cultish ritual and a virulent hierarchy. He preys on the gullible. His flock become his hostages.

Religious authority also secures the narcissist's Narcissistic Supply. His coreligionists, members of his congregation, his parish, his constituency, his audience - are transformed into loyal and stable Sources of Narcissistic Supply. They obey his commands, heed his admonitions, follow his creed, admire his personality, applaud his personal traits, satisfy his needs (sometimes even his carnal desires), revere and idolise him.

Moreover, being a part of a "bigger thing" is very gratifying narcissistically. Being a particle of God, being immersed in His grandeur, experiencing His power and blessings first hand, communing with him - are all Sources of unending Narcissistic Supply. The narcissist becomes God by observing His commandments, following His instructions, loving Him, obeying Him, succumbing to Him, merging with Him, communicating with Him - or even by defying him (the bigger the narcissist's enemy - the more grandiosely important the narcissist feels).

Like everything else in the narcissist's life, he mutates God into a kind of inverted narcissist. God becomes his dominant Source of Supply. He forms a personal relationship with this overwhelming and overpowering entity - in order to overwhelm and overpower others. He becomes God vicariously, by the proxy of his relationship with Him. He idealises God, then devalues Him, then abuses Him. This is the classic narcissistic pattern and even God himself cannot escape it.

First published on the Suite 101 Narcissistic Personality Disorders Topic.

Return

The Narcissist and Social Institutions

The narcissist is prone to magical thinking. He regards himself in terms of "being chosen" or of "being destined for greatness". He believes that he has a "direct line" to God, even, perversely, that God "serves" him in certain junctions and conjunctures of his life, through divine intervention. He believes that his life is of such momentous importance, that it is micro-managed by God. The narcissist likes to play God to his human environment. In short, narcissism and religion go well together, because religion allows the narcissist to feel unique.

This is a private case of a more general phenomenon. The narcissist likes to belong to groups or to frameworks of allegiance. He derives easy and constantly available Narcissistic Supply from them. Within them and from their members he is certain to garner attention, to gain adulation, to be castigated or praised. His False Self is bound to be reflected by his colleagues, co-members, or fellows.

This is no mean feat and it cannot be guaranteed in other circumstances. Hence the narcissist's fanatic and proud emphasis of his membership. If a military man, he shows off his impressive array of medals, his impeccably pressed uniform, the status symbols of his rank. If a clergyman, he is overly devout and orthodox and places great emphasis on the proper conduct of rites, rituals and ceremonies.

The narcissist develops a reverse (benign) form of paranoia: he feels constantly watched over by senior members of his group or frame of reference, the subject of permanent (avuncular) criticism, the centre of attention. If a religious man, he calls it divine providence. This self-centred perception also caters to the narcissist's streak of grandiosity, proving that he is, indeed, worthy of such incessant and detailed attention, supervision and intervention.

From this mental junction, the way is short to entertaining the delusion that God (or the equivalent institutional authority) is an active participant in the narcissist's life in which constant intervention by Him is a key feature. God is subsumed in a larger picture, that of the narcissist's destiny and mission. God serves this cosmic plan by making it possible.

Indirectly, therefore, God is perceived by the narcissist to be at his service. Moreover, in a process of holographic appropriation, the narcissist views himself as a microcosm of his affiliation, of his group, or his frame of reference. The narcissist is likely to say that he IS the army, the nation, the people, the struggle, history, or (a part of) God.

As opposed to healthier people, the narcissist believes that he both represents and embodies his class, his people, his race, history, his God, his art - or anything else he feels a part of. This is why individual narcissists feel completely comfortable to assume roles usually reserved to groups of people or to some transcendental, divine (or other), authority.

This kind of "enlargement" or "inflation" also sits well with the narcissist's all-pervasive feelings of omnipotence, omnipresence, and omniscience. In playing God, for instance, the narcissist is completely convinced that he is merely being himself. The narcissist does not hesitate to put people's lives or fortunes at risk. He preserves his sense of infallibility in the face of mistakes and misjudgements by distorting the facts, by evoking mitigating or attenuating circumstances, by repressing memories, or by simply lying.

In the overall design of things, small setbacks and defeats matter little, says the narcissist. The narcissist is haunted by the feeling that he is possessed of a mission, of a destiny, that he is part of fate, of history. He is convinced that his uniqueness is purposeful, that he is meant to lead, to chart new ways, to innovate, to modernise, to reform, to set precedents, or to create from scratch.

Every act of the narcissist is perceived by him to be significant, every utterance of momentous consequence, every thought of revolutionary calibre. He feels part of a grand design, a world plan and the frame of affiliation, the group, of which he is a member, must be commensurately grand. Its proportions and properties must resonate with his. Its characteristics must justify his and its ideology must conform to his pre-conceived opinions and prejudices.

In short: the group must magnify the narcissist, echo and amplify his life, his views, his knowledge, and his personal history. This intertwining, this enmeshing of individual and collective, is what makes the narcissist the most devout and loyal of all its members.

The narcissist is always the most fanatical, the most extreme, the most dangerous adherent. At stake is never merely the preservation of his group – but his very own survival. As with other Narcissistic Supply Sources, once the group is no longer instrumental – the narcissist loses all interest in it, devalues it and ignores it.

In extreme cases, he might even wish to destroy it (as a punishment or revenge for its incompetence in securing his emotional needs). Narcissists switch groups and ideologies with ease (as they do partners, spouses and value systems). In this respect, narcissists are narcissists first and members of their groups only in the second place.

Return

Guide to Coping with Narcissists and Psychopaths

Save for later reference! Forward to interested parties and relevant discussion and mailing groups!

Click with your mouse on the links (the blue text).

How to Cope with Narcissistic and Psychopathic Abusers
http://samvak.tripod.com/faq4.html
http://samvak.tripod.com/abusefamily19.html
http://samvak.tripod.com/abusefamily20.html
http://samvak.tripod.com/npdtips.html
http://samvak.tripod.com/5.html
http://samvak.tripod.com/faq80.html
http://samvak.tripod.com/4.html
http://samvak.tripod.com/faq75.html
http://samvak.tripod.com/journal56.html
http://samvak.tripod.com/journal68.html

Strategies for Coping with Abusers (General)
http://samvak.tripod.com/abuse.html
http://samvak.tripod.com/abuse3.html
http://samvak.tripod.com/abuse17.html
http://samvak.tripod.com/abuse19.html
http://samvak.tripod.com/abuse20.html
http://samvak.tripod.com/abuse21.html
http://samvak.tripod.com/abuse21a.html

http://samvak.tripod.com/abuse21b.html
http://samvak.tripod.com/abuse12.html
http://samvak.tripod.com/abuse13.html
http://samvak.tripod.com/abuse5.html
http://samvak.tripod.com/abuse6.html
http://samvak.tripod.com/abusefamily13.html
http://samvak.tripod.com/abusefamily5.html
http://samvak.tripod.com/abusefamily6.html
http://samvak.tripod.com/abusefamily8.html

Working with the System and with Professionals
http://samvak.tripod.com/abusefamily10.html
http://samvak.tripod.com/abusefamily11.html
http://samvak.tripod.com/abusefamily12.html

How to Cope with Stalkers and Paranoids
http://samvak.tripod.com/abuse18.html
http://samvak.tripod.com/abuse15.html
http://samvak.tripod.com/abuse16.html
http://samvak.tripod.com/abusefamily14.html
http://samvak.tripod.com/abusefamily16.html
http://samvak.tripod.com/abusefamily17.html
http://samvak.tripod.com/abusefamily18.html

Return

THE AUTHOR

Shmuel (Sam) Vaknin

Curriculum Vitae

Born in 1961 in Qiryat-Yam, Israel.

Served in the Israeli Defence Force (1979-1982) in training and education units.

Education

1970-1978: Completed nine semesters in the Technion – Israel Institute of Technology, Haifa.

1982-3: Ph.D. in Philosophy (dissertation: "Time Asymmetry Revisited") – Pacific Western University, **California**, USA.

1982-5: Graduate of numerous courses in Finance Theory and International Trading in the UK and USA.

Certified E-Commerce Concepts Analyst by Brainbench.

Certified in Psychological Counselling Techniques by Brainbench.

Certified Financial Analyst by Brainbench.

Full proficiency in Hebrew and in English.

Business Experience

1980 to 1983

Founder and co-owner of a chain of computerised information kiosks in Tel-Aviv, Israel.

1982 to 1985

Senior positions with the Nessim D. Gaon Group of Companies in Geneva, Paris and New-York (NOGA and APROFIM SA):

– Chief Analyst of Edible Commodities in the Group's Headquarters in Switzerland
– Manager of the Research and Analysis Division
– Manager of the Data Processing Division
– Project Manager of the Nigerian Computerised Census
– Vice President in charge of RND and Advanced Technologies
– Vice President in charge of Sovereign Debt Financing

1985 to 1986

Represented Canadian Venture Capital Funds in Israel.

1986 to 1987

General Manager of IPE Ltd. in London. The firm financed international multi-lateral countertrade and leasing transactions.

1988 to 1990

Co-founder and Director of "Mikbats-Tesuah", a portfolio management firm based in Tel-Aviv. Activities included large-scale portfolio management, underwriting, forex trading and general financial advisory services.

1990 to Present

Freelance consultant to many of Israel's Blue-Chip firms, mainly on issues related to the capital markets in Israel, Canada, the UK and the USA.

Consultant to foreign RND ventures and to Governments on macro-economic matters.

Freelance journalist in various media in the United States.

1990 to 1995

President of the Israel chapter of the Professors World Peace Academy (PWPA) and (briefly) Israel representative of the "Washington Times".

1993 to 1994

Co-owner and Director of many business enterprises:

– The Omega and Energy Air-Conditioning Concern
– AVP Financial Consultants
– Handiman Legal Services
   Total annual turnover of the group: 10 million USD.

Co-owner, Director and Finance Manager of COSTI Ltd. – Israel's largest computerised information vendor and developer. Raised funds through a series of private placements locally in the USA, Canada and London.

1993 to 1996

Publisher and Editor of a Capital Markets Newsletter distributed by subscription only to dozens of subscribers countrywide.

In a legal precedent in 1995 – studied in business schools and law faculties across Israel – was tried for his role in an attempted takeover of Israel's Agriculture Bank.

Was interned in the State School of Prison Wardens.

Managed the Central School Library, wrote, published and lectured on various occasions.

Managed the Internet and International News Department of an Israeli mass media group, "Ha-Tikshoret and Namer".

Assistant in the Law Faculty in Tel-Aviv University (to Prof. S.G. Shoham).

1996 to 1999

Financial consultant to leading businesses in Macedonia, Russia and the Czech Republic.

Economic commentator in "Nova Makedonija", "Dnevnik", "Makedonija Denes", "Izvestia", "Argumenti i Fakti", "The Middle East Times", "The New Presence", "Central Europe Review", and other periodicals, and in the economic programs on various channels of Macedonian Television.

Chief Lecturer in courses in Macedonia organised by the Agency of Privatization, by the Stock Exchange, and by the Ministry of Trade.

1999 to 2002

Economic Advisor to the Government of the Republic of Macedonia and to the Ministry of Finance.

2001 to 2003

Senior Business Correspondent for United Press International (UPI).

2007 -

Associate Editor, Global Politician

Founding Analyst, The Analyst Network

Contributing Writer, The American Chronicle Media Group

Expert, Self-growth.com

2007-2008

Columnist and analyst in "Nova Makedonija", "Fokus", and "Kapital" (Macedonian papers and newsweeklies).

2008-

Member of the Steering Committee for the Advancement of Healthcare in the Republic of Macedonia

Advisor to the Minister of Health of Macedonia

Seminars and lectures on economic issues in various forums in Macedonia.

Web and Journalistic Activities

Author of extensive Web sites in:

– Psychology ("Malignant Self Love") - An Open Directory Cool Site for 8 years.

– Philosophy ("Philosophical Musings"),

– Economics and Geopolitics ("World in Conflict and Transition").

Owner of the Narcissistic Abuse Study Lists and the Abusive Relationships Newsletter (more than 6,000 members).

Owner of the Economies in Conflict and Transition Study List , the Toxic Relationships Study List, and the Links and Factoid Study List.

Editor of mental health disorders and Central and Eastern Europe categories in various Web directories (Open Directory, Search Europe, Mentalhelp.net).

Editor of the Personality Disorders, Narcissistic Personality Disorder, the Verbal and Emotional Abuse, and the Spousal (Domestic) Abuse and Violence topics on Suite 101 and Bellaonline.

Columnist and commentator in "The New Presence", United Press International (UPI), InternetContent, eBookWeb, PopMatters, Global Politician, The Analyst Network, Conservative Voice, The American Chronicle Media Group, eBookNet.org, and "Central Europe Review".

Publications and Awards

"Managing Investment Portfolios in States of Uncertainty", Limon Publishers, Tel-Aviv, 1988

"The Gambling Industry", Limon Publishers, Tel-Aviv, 1990

"Requesting My Loved One – Short Stories", Yedioth Aharonot, Tel-Aviv, 1997

"The Suffering of Being Kafka" (electronic book of Hebrew and English Short Fiction), Prague, 1998-2004

"The Macedonian Economy at a Crossroads – On the Way to a Healthier Economy" (dialogues with Nikola Gruevski), Skopje, 1998

"The Exporters' Pocketbook", Ministry of Trade, Republic of Macedonia, Skopje, 1999

"Malignant Self Love – Narcissism Revisited", Narcissus Publications, Prague, 1999-2007 (Read excerpts - click here)

The Narcissism, Psychopathy, and Abuse in Relationships Series (E-books regarding relationships with abusive narcissists and psychopaths), Prague, 1999-2010

Personality Disorders Revisited (e-book about personality disorders), Prague, 2007

"After the Rain – How the West Lost the East", Narcissus Publications in association with Central Europe Review/CEENMI, Prague and Skopje, 2000

Winner of numerous awards, among them Israel's Council of Culture and Art Prize for Maiden Prose (1997), The Rotary Club Award for Social Studies (1976), and the Bilateral Relations Studies Award of the American Embassy in Israel (1978).

Hundreds of professional articles in all fields of finance and economics, and numerous articles dealing with geopolitical and political economic issues published in both print and Web periodicals in many countries.

[Many appearances in the electronic media](#) on subjects in philosophy and the sciences, and concerning economic matters.

Write to Me:
palma@unet.com.mk
narcissisticabuse-owner@yahoogroups.com

My Web Sites:

Economy/Politics:

http://ceeandbalkan.tripod.com/

Psychology:

http://www.narcissistic-abuse.com/

Philosophy:

http://philosophos.tripod.com/

Poetry:

http://samvak.tripod.com/contents.html

Fiction:

http://samvak.tripod.com/sipurim.html

Return

Abused? Stalked? Harassed? Bullied? Victimized?
Afraid? Confused? Need HELP? DO SOMETHING ABOUT IT!

Had a Narcissistic Parent?
Married to a Narcissist – or Divorcing One?
Afraid your children will turn out the same?
Want to cope with this pernicious, baffling condition?
OR
Are You a Narcissist – or suspect that You are one...
This book will teach you how to...
Cope, Survive, and Protect Your Loved Ones!
You should read...

"Malignant Self Love - Narcissism Revisited"
The EIGHTH, REVISED PRINTING (January 2007) is now available!

Nine additional e-books, All NEW Editions, JUST RELEASED!!!
Malignant Self Love, Toxic Relationships,
Pathological Narcissism, Coping with Divorce,
The Narcissist and Psychopath in the Workplace – and MORE!!!

Click on this link to purchase the PRINT BOOK and/or the NINE E-BOOKS
http://www.narcissistic-abuse.com/thebook.html

Sam Vaknin published the EIGHTH, REVISED IMPRESSION of his book about relationships with abusive narcissists, **"Malignant Self Love - Narcissism Revisited"**.

The book deals with the Narcissistic Personality Disorder and its effects on the narcissist and his nearest and dearest – in 102 frequently asked questions and two essays – a total of 600 pages!

Print Edition from BARNES AND NOBLE and AMAZON

Barnes and Noble – "Malignant Self Love – Narcissism Revisited" EIGHTH, Revised, Impression (January 2007)

ON SALE starting at $40.45 !!!

INSTEAD OF the publisher's list price of $54.95 (including shipping and handling)!!!

That's more than $14 off the publisher's list price!!!!

Click on this link to purchase the paper edition:

http://search.barnesandnoble.com/bookSearch/isbnInquiry.asp?r=1&ISBN=9788023833843

And from **Amazon.com** – Click on this link:

http://www.amazon.com/exec/obidos/tg/detail/-/8023833847/

Print Edition from the PUBLISHER

The previous revised impression of Sam Vaknin's "Malignant Self - Love - Narcissism Revisited".

Comes with an exclusive BONUS PACK (not available through Barnes and Noble or Amazon).

Contains the entire text: essays, frequently asked questions and appendices regarding pathological narcissism and the Narcissistic Personality Disorder (NPD).

The publisher charges the full list price – but throws into the bargain a bonus pack with hundreds of additional pages and seven free e-books.

Click on this link:

http://www.ccnow.com/cgi-local/cart.cgi?vaksam_MSL

Free excerpts from the EIGHTH, Revised Impression of **"Malignant Self Love - Narcissism Revisited"** are available as well as a free NEW EDITION of the Narcissism Book of Quotes

Click on this link to download the files:

http://www.narcissistic-abuse.com/freebooks.html

"After the Rain - How the West Lost the East"

The history, cultures, societies, and economies of countries in transition in the Balkans.

Click on this link to purchase this print book:

http://www.ccnow.com/cgi-local/cart.cgi?vaksam_ATR

Electronic Books (e-books) from the Publisher

An *electronic book* is a computer file, sent to you as an attachment to an e-mail message. Just save it to your hard disk and click on the file to open, read, and learn!

1. **"Malignant Self Love - Narcissism Revisited"**
   Eighth, Revised Edition (January 2007)

   The e-book version of Sam Vaknin's "Malignant Self - Love - Narcissism Revisited". Contains the entire text: essays, frequently asked questions (FAQs) and appendices regarding pathological narcissism and the Narcissistic Personality Disorder (NPD).

   Click on this link to purchase the e-book:

   http://www.ccnow.com/cgi-local/cart.cgi?vaksam_MSL-EBOOK

2. **"The Narcissism, Psychopathy, and Abuse in Relationships Series"** Eighth, Revised Edition (July 2010)

   NINE e-books (more than 3000 pages), including the full text of "Malignant Self Love - Narcissism Revisited", regarding Pathological Narcissism, relationships with abusive narcissists and psychopaths, and the Narcissistic Personality Disorder (NPD).

   Click on this link to purchase the EIGHT e-books:

   http://www.ccnow.com/cgi-local/cart.cgi?vaksam_SERIES

3. **"Toxic Relationships - Abuse and its Aftermath"**
   Fourth Edition (February 2006)

   How to identify abuse, cope with it, survive it, and deal with your abuser and with the system in divorce and custody issues.

   Click on this link to purchase the e-book:

   http://www.ccnow.com/cgi-local/cart.cgi?vaksam_ABUSE

4. **"The Narcissist and Psychopath in the Workplace"**
   (September 2006)

   Identify abusers, bullies, and stalkers in the workplace (bosses, colleagues, suppliers, and authority figures) and learn how to cope with them effectively.

   Click on this link to purchase the e-book:

   http://www.ccnow.com/cgi-local/cart.cgi?vaksam_WORKPLACE

5. **"Abusive Relationships Workbook"** (February 2006)

   Self-assessment questionnaires, tips, and tests for victims of abusers, batterers, and stalkers in various types of relationships.

   Click on this link to purchase the e-book:

   http://www.ccnow.com/cgi-local/cart.cgi?vaksam_WORKBOOK

6. **"Pathological Narcissism FAQs"**
   Eighth, Revised Edition (January 2007)

   Dozens of Frequently Asked Questions regarding Pathological Narcissism, relationships with abusive narcissists, and the Narcissistic Personality Disorder.

   Click on this link to purchase the e-book:

   http://www.ccnow.com/cgi-local/cart.cgi?vaksam_FAQS

7. **"The World of the Narcissist"**
   Eighth, Revised Edition (January 2007)

   A book-length psychodynamic study of pathological narcissism, relationships with abusive narcissists, and the Narcissistic Personality Disorder, using a new vocabulary.

   Click on this link to purchase the e-book:

   http://www.ccnow.com/cgi-local/cart.cgi?vaksam_ESSAY

8. **"Excerpts from the Archives of the Narcissism List"**

Hundreds of excerpts from the archives of the Narcissistic Abuse Study List regarding Pathological Narcissism, relationships with abusive narcissists, and the Narcissistic Personality Disorder (NPD).

Click on this link to purchase the e-book:

http://www.ccnow.com/cgi-local/cart.cgi?vaksam_EXCERPTS

9. **"Diary of a Narcissist"** (November 2005)

The anatomy of one man's mental illness – its origins, its unfolding, its outcomes.

Click on this link to purchase the e-book:

http://www.ccnow.com/cgi-local/cart.cgi?vaksam_JOURNAL

10. *"The Narcissist and Psychopath in Therapy"*

Can narcissists and psychopaths be cured? Can their behaviour be modified? How are these mental health disorders diagnosed?

Buy it from the publisher - click on this link:

http://www.ccnow.com/cgi-local/cart.cgi?vaksam_THERAPY

11. **"After the Rain - How the West Lost the East"**

The history, cultures, societies, and economies of countries in transition in the Balkans.

Click on this link to purchase the e-book:

http://www.ccnow.com/cgi-local/cart.cgi?vaksam_ATR-EBOOK

Download Free Electronic Books

Click on this link:

http://www.narcissistic-abuse.com/freebooks.html

More about the Books and Additional Resources

The Eighth, Revised Impression (January 2007) of the Print Edition of **"Malignant Self Love - Narcissism Revisited"** includes:
- The full text of "Malignant Self Love - Narcissism Revisited"
- The full text of 102 Frequently Asked Questions and Answers

- Covering all the dimensions of Pathological Narcissism and Abuse in Relationships
- An Essay – The Narcissist's point of view
- Bibliography
- 600 printed pages in a quality paper book
- Digital Bonus Pack! (available only when you purchase the previous edition from the Publisher) – Bibliography, three e-books, additional FAQs, appendices and more – hundreds of additional pages!

Testimonials and Additional Resources

You can read Readers' Reviews at the Barnes and Noble Web page dedicated to "Malignant Self Love" – HERE:

http://search.barnesandnoble.com/bookSearch/isbnInquiry.asp?r=1&ISBN=9788023833843

Dozens of Links and Resources

Click on these links:

The Narcissistic Abuse Study List

http://groups.yahoo.com/group/narcissisticabuse

The Toxic Relationships Study List

http://groups.yahoo.com/group/toxicrelationships

Abusive Relationships Newsletter

http://groups.google.com/group/narcissisticabuse

Participate in Discussions about Abusive Relationships - click on these links:

http://narcissisticabuse.ning.com/

http://www.runboard.com/bnarcissisticabuserecovery

http://thepsychopath.freeforums.org/

The Narcissistic Abuse Study List

http://health.groups.yahoo.com/group/narcissisticabuse/

The Toxic Relationships Study List

http://groups.yahoo.com/group/toxicrelationships

Abusive Relationships Newsletter

http://groups.google.com/group/narcissisticabuse/

Archived discussion threads - click on these links:

http://personalitydisorders.suite101.com/discussions.cfm

http://www.suite101.com/discussions.cfm/verbal_emotional_abuse

http://www.suite101.com/discussuions.cfm/spousal_domestic_abuse

Links to Therapist Directories, Psychological Tests, NPD Resources, Support Groups for Narcissists and Their Victims, and Tutorials

http://health.groups.yahoo.com/group/narcissisticabuse/message/5458

Support Groups for Victims of Narcissists and Narcissists

http://dmoz.org/Health/Mental_Health/Disorders/Personality/Narcissistic

BE WELL, SAFE AND WARM WHEREVER YOU ARE!

Sam Vaknin

Malignant Self Love
Narcissism Revisited

The Book

"Narcissists live in a state of constant rage, repressed aggression, envy and hatred. They firmly believe that everyone is like them. As a result, they are paranoid, aggressive, haughty and erratic. Narcissists are forever in pursuit of Narcissistic Supply.
They know no past or future, are not constrained by any behavioural consistency, 'rules' of conduct or moral considerations. You signal to a narcissist that you are a willing source - and he is bound to extract his supply from you.
This is a reflex.
He would have reacted absolutely the same to any other source. If what is needed to obtain supply from you is intimations of intimacy - he will supply them liberally."

This book is comprised of two parts.
The first part contains 102 Frequently Asked Questions related to the various aspects of pathological narcissism, relationships with abusive narcissists, and the Narcissistic Personality Disorder (NPD).
The second part is an exposition of the various psychodynamic theories regarding pathological narcissism and a proposed new vocabulary.

The Author

Sam Vaknin was born in Israel in 1961. A financial consultant and columnist, he lived (and published) in 12 countries.
He is a published and awarded author of short fiction and reference and an editor of mental health categories in various Web directories. This is his twelfth book.

www.ingramcontent.com/pod-product-compliance
Lightning Source LLC
Chambersburg PA
CBHW020551220526
45463CB00006B/2258